Sunlight Through Bullet Holes

Poems
(that will live)

jessica Care moore

Moment of Silence

dedicated to the lifework of

Amiri Baraka
Jasmine Bailey
Jayne Cortez
Gil Scott Herron
John Watusi Branch

In Loving Memory of
Thomas Davis Moore
Rakiba Brown
Rashan Hilson
Christopher Moore
Uncle Graham

we continue.....

Sunlight Through Bullet Holes

Editor: Aurora Harris
Cover and Back Cover Art: jessica Care moore and Piper Carter
Inside Photo: "Books Are Sexy": Piper Carter
Book Design: Michael Angelo Chester

Moore Black Press Publishing Inc.
The Jess Care Moore Foundation
1401 W. Fort St. #442488
Detroit, MI 48244

www.mooreblackpress.com
Author bookings/book orders: mooreblackpress@gmail.com

All paintings by jessica Care moore,
*Amiri Baraka Painting by Michael Angelo Chester.

Library of Congress Cataloging in Publication Data
(Contact MBP)

TABLE OF CONTENTS

I Take Full Responsibility For My Actions...

Cashing in…
poet with sky miles
I wish I could write this poem in Chinese
the cat in the window
haikus
deep breath
traveling moon
When the day begins and ends with fireworks

no encore

no encore
When I write there is light

sunlight through bullet holes

sunlight through bullet holes
L'Union Fait La Force
for tea
flawless
When Poets
a poem saved my life
i needed to write a love poem

bio

introduction

Mommy, eyes are better than mirrors

—*King Thomas, 6 years old*

Describing art as jazz, poems, or performance is just a way for people to put art into boxes. Miles Davis called jazz an "uncle tom" word. I am a writer. I write poems, prose, letters, dialogue; scripts, plays, music, and personal truth. I resisted the label of spoken word most of my writing career.

Sunlight Through Bullet Holes is a book with a sound track. The metaphoric metronome for these poems is what some people may simply call jazz. Years ago in Atlanta, I performed with a quartet whose member said the way I read my poetry reminded him of Miles because I took deep breaths and I kept going until there was no breath left. With my affinity to the power, growl, and lyrics of Miles' former rocker wife, Betty Davis, and my love for rock and roll, I never thought deeply into the comparison until now.

When I read my poems, I often feel like I'm "going away." Many of my artist friends have spoken to me about this out of body type of experience on stage. I've seen it countless times with my brilliant friend Roger Guenveur Smith as he transformed into Huey P Newton and Rodney King. The goal is to recover and find a way back to reality.

Ain't nothing simple bout jazz, poetry, or love. I have held the light of love in my mouth like a firefly in a jar full of holes. Captive. Afraid. Open. Fearless. Always flying, even when wings were tired and mouth was full of sand.

Here comes love, in the form of water...The blown trumpet...The tug on a string. Muddy. Water. Love.

When Etta James died, I cried as if I'd lost an auntie I meant to call but didn't. When I heard Whitney Houston had passed, the way she passed, I was with the legendary Roy Ayers in Kansas City for a performance at the American Jazz Museum. It was devastating news. Beautiful poet Louis Reyes Rivera would die soon after our show together there. I performed "You Want Poems" with Roy and it brought me to tears, and it does every time every since that moment.

I'd met Whitney Houston years ago when I was a cast member in the Broadway musical *Born To Sing Mama 3* by Vy Higgenson. Whitney came to our opening night because her friend CeCe Winans was one of the stars of the show. After the performance she said, "I liked your poems," and I replied, "I was really nervous, I don't think I was my best." Whitney, in all her beauty and New Jersey grace said, "If you were perfect today, how are you gonna be better tomorrow?"

I loved her immensely ever since that moment.

The pain of women artists inspires all. We play their music repeatedly after they are buried in the ground. We celebrate their genius, their misery, their heartbreaks, their tears.

This body of work will forever be connected to music. My first real recording project, *Black Tea – The Legend of Jessi James*.

Still, I wanted the text to have its own space on the page, bound by a spine. Books are like women. Filled up with so much love & imagination. Our stems, our complicated perfect bind holding all our pages together.

Men are sometimes just the page numbers. Breaths between chapters. A marker for the just now. A bookmark to bloodshed. A love lost. A heart aching to be understood. The ricochet of the bullet against the panel of our shot-gun Midwest houses.

This little light

sunlight

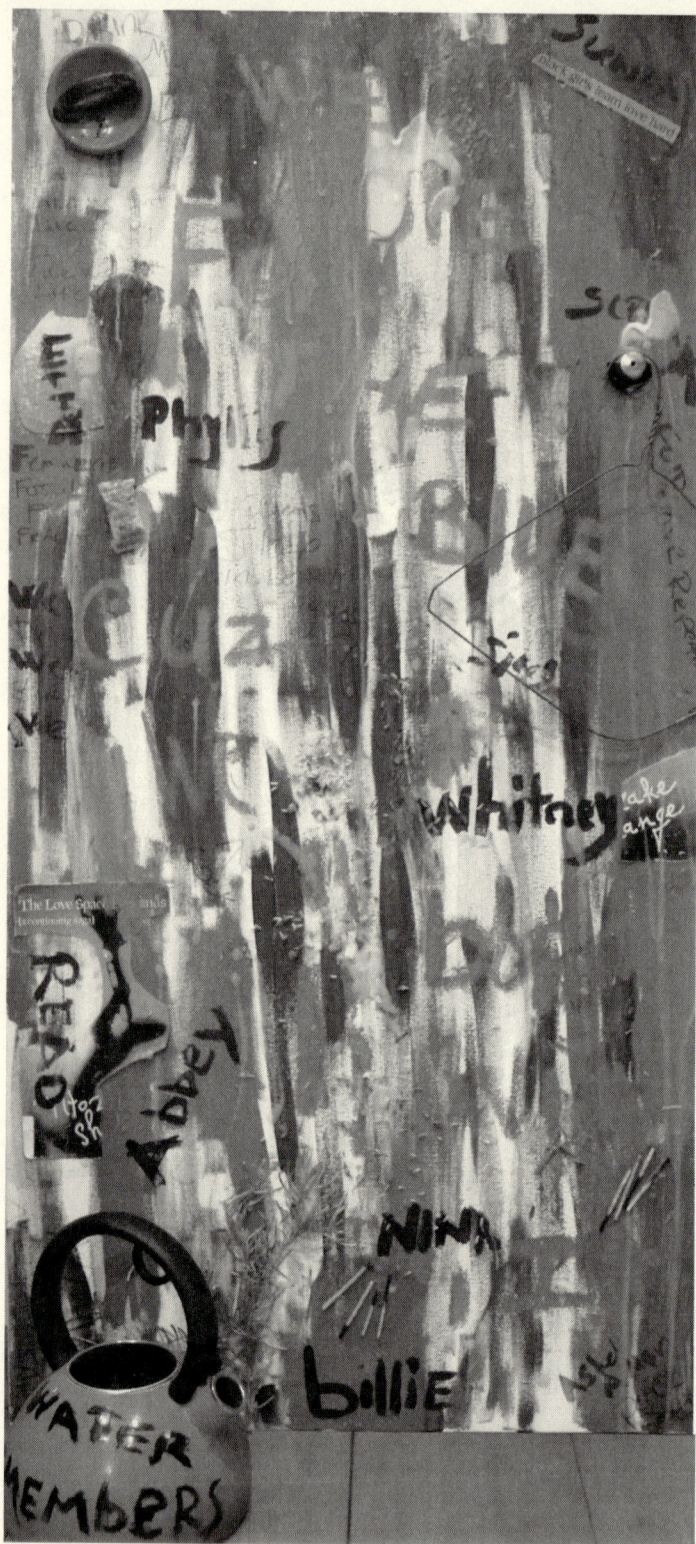

Sunlight Through Bullet Holes

it ain't like we don't

for Etta James. Haiku as Prayer

it ain't like we don't
like loving. we die for blues
cuz we born with it
it ain't like we don't
like loving. we die for blues
cuz we born with it

madness. the veil of
the mic. our voice flight
memories don't lie

we die of broken
hearts. transparent art. they clap.
pretend to be smart

proof of existence.
feminine fossil for frauds
we cry. we birth. we

deliberate smile.
forced on our mouths. open.
history pours out.

it ain't like we don't
love candles. or ashes lit.
we the flame. smoking.

america holds
our hearts of royalty. owns
our essence. rebels.

music is not yours

to take. stone rolling. blues runs
deep in these thick veins

the beautiful ones
alone with the notes. dancing
inside a body.
spirit fills the void.
laughter measured. broke. holy
bread. we melt on tongues.
at last. rock & roll
gets on it's knees. thanks mama
shall come first. they say.

it ain't like we pray
to a different God. you know?
amen. ashe. peace.

wonder what they do
with our bones. build a shrine. queens
sleep in death. i guess.

our legs still shake. shed
off skin. borrow wind as breath.
lucy has daughters.

fatherless. but still
daddy meant the world. absence
makes art grow fonder.

blind is a blessing
when u got eyes everywhere
looking for your flaws.

etta, it's sunday
as i write this. 12:09
kinda love. these tears.

it ain't like we dream
of knights. in armor. shining
not since music. played.

at a wedding. stop.
pain inspires genius tongue.
i made that man. great.

know your place. brown girl
don't sing that truth to loud. scream!
it through the speakers.
it ain't like we don't like
loving. we die for the blues.
cuz we born with it.

I was given the nickname "jessi james" in Brooklyn in 1995. There is a debate over who gave it to me. But, it was the name i was called by my two dear friends, Talib Kweli and Dante Smith aka Mos Def and now Yasin Bey. They were both "Black Stars" in the making. I was a native cadillac riding NYC subway trains. "Jessi James" came to brooklyn with guns drawn & motor city muscle, but she really just wanted love. they wanted poems. they always want poems.

⭐ **you**want**poems** ⭐

This poem was recorded for my music project, Black Tea. Jon Dixon wrote the music. Roy Ayers added the Vibes. Jose James croons all over the track. This is for you JJ. You are a gift to music.

when u are a woman
when u are brown
when u are brave
when u walk over glass like water
when u know your eyes are
borrowed like time.
when u peel off your skin
for the very first time

fear is never in style
in the mecca of the blue
fear never lives
in the gut of the new

you want poems
& i just want to build my home
you want poems
& i just want love in my hands
you want poems
& i'm not interested in fans
you love me inside my magic
& i just want u you to see
you already had it.

Sunlight Through Bullet Holes

it is in the telling when someone asks
it is the way he holds the glass
licks the surface. examines without
touching.
it is the way our energy takes over rooms
it is the subtle conversation
it is the freedom of emancipated language
it is in the words scribbled inside my skin
it is the curve of the line. the beauty of the lies
stories passed down thru generations of
pain and pride
ocean and tide
it's water remembers water returns

african mermaids blending with dark sand
is is the danger of the dance
the upright heart of the bass
the dice roll drum experiment
the cymbal tease
the last laugh the addiction
to this moment.

where else do i put it

?

don't know where to put it
place it. bury it. deep in my chest.
back of my throat. where shld i hide it.
on this stage. shld i give it to you.
here is my honesty. my work undressed.
legs stretched across piano.
traded like cattle. raped like animal.
left for dead. sucked dry for inspiration
in love with the idea of living long enough
to simply write about it. push it out my body

and watch my son slowly grow into it.
you said you wanted a poem.

now what/chu gon' do wit it
?

huh

whitney
etta
abbey
billie
nina
phyllis

how much time you got?

i'm a body of clocks
i'm the master of mics
i'm the metaphor for survival
i am the gold they use to build their
churches

a beautiful idea to flirt with

but who shall i marry?
the moonlight
the sunrise
the white dove? the wolf?
an eastern wind?
this music?
a prayer

how many babies we gon make
inside a song?
which revolution which nation

shall we rule?
the island of the spirit world
the beauty of the believers
the carpenters/the men who
build the dream & place u
on the frontline of their planet

one day the stars will line up
between breath & ink & voice
some place between reality & choice

it is the danger of the dance
the upright bass of the heart
the dice roll drum experiment
the cymbal tease
the last laugh/ the addiction

to this moment.

poem before the end of the world

if the sky falls and covers us like an ocean
if the sun turns cold and light abandons our hearts
i wld wrap my arms around the space left behind
and know it was you.

what if i wrote a poem
pulled back from the corner
of your jazz/blues mouth. a book
i sometimes re-read
to remind me that real lives
make these stories

there is so much truth
in the softest places.

what if i believed there was
no such thing as dead
what is our commitment
what is written + what is said

how long do i have you for
maybe just till 4.

is that enough time

?

to make something revolutionary
is that enough time to change
the inevitable clock.

you. my book/mark
waiting for me to open

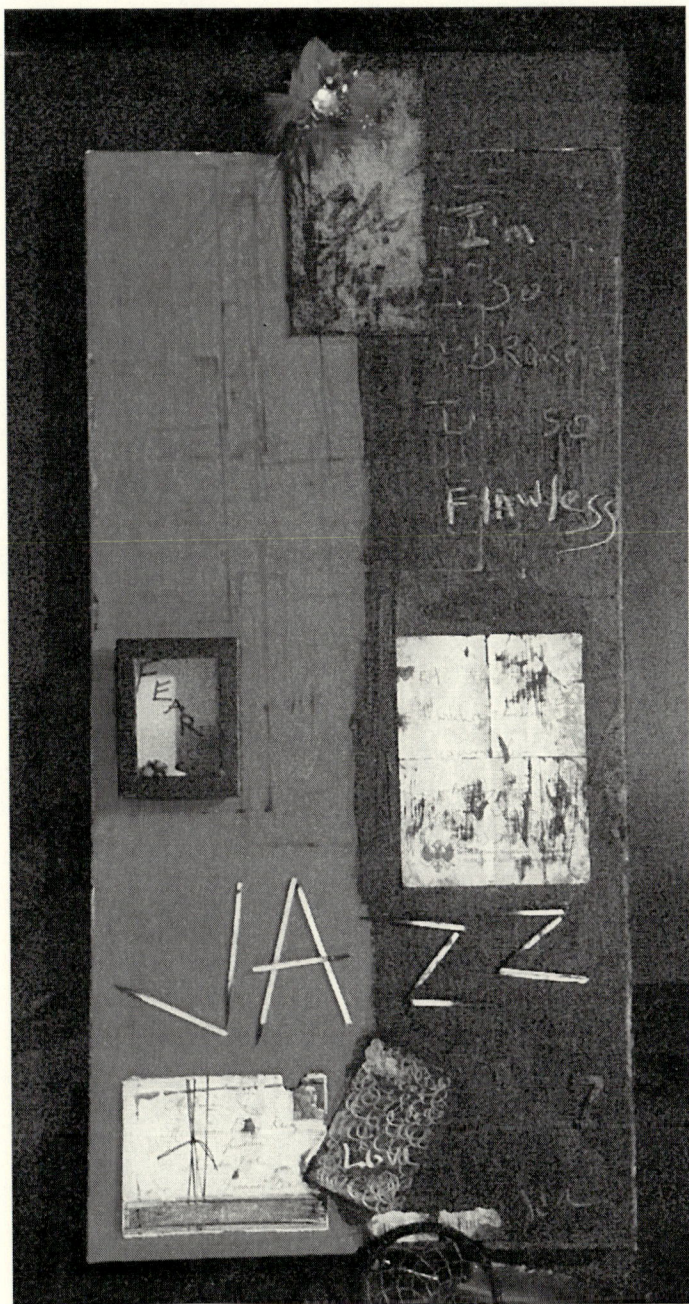

Poem Before The End of The World
mixed media. acrylic.
matches, personal notes, memories, fear, love, jazz.

to the right page. the right moment
i lie my body down inside your favorite
lines from toni
remember every word /you told me.

our kiss is the 14th line
somewhere there is snow & i'm
skating away on a joni river
there is a yes on the other side

of every no.

love used to be just ink on paper
we so sophisticated (now)
love used to be just ink on paper
we so unconventional (now)

we so old we new
we so old we new
we so old we knew.

your eyes look like an ancestor
my spirit flew through

is this room through with you

?

i got something i've been
meaning to tell you
for 400 years.
ossie had ruby
malcolm had betty
king had coretta
& all we have is fear

and i just want a few seconds
to make a little history
with you.
take in a little mystery
with you.

i'm drinking red i'm laughing loud
i'm so broken i'm so flawless
i'm in the bed waiting for the earth
to call us.

crum/ba/lin.

i'm watching walls
fall down. around us. my stolen heart hidden
on a dusty shelf. i love the
sound of suddenly being found.
this is my poem
before the end of the world
this is my poem inspired by
the children of bahia
the sunset of soweto
here's to brooklyn bridges
detroit love letters

& blacktop salvation
sidewalk chalk and liberation
names carved in trees
six degrees & hollywood dreams

this is a song
for lovers. this is a poem
you bury in your finest gear

when the sun is done
when the sun is done

when the southern sun is done
when the moon is cold
when music is the only thing
left to hold
i will listen to your voice so old.
what if i wrote you
my very last poem

?

what if this short hour just saved me?
armageddon is for lovers baby
when the sun is done
with us. when your smile is no
longer in a rush.
i'll simply give what God gave me
to give.
& write more poems so we
can live.
live live
live live live
love.

Naima

invisible & infamous

did coltrane know
it wuz rebel music?
wld he have given us permission
to hold him in this light?

this is not my Coltrane poem

--------------------------or is it?

denial is an art form.
truth is blood & water.
digging under notes.
an excavation is dirty
unyielding, wrapped in Moroccan silk
pulled gently behind the ears.

a tea kettle ringing. knuckles against a window.
a cutting. a black scream. a set of eyes.
a series of memories. a disappearing act.
a re-discovery. a writing out of history.
a wiping out of refrain.

bridges.

she crossed them.
she bore them.

where are her critics?

no one is checking her tracks, her arms, for context?
what percentage for soul?
how much publishing for breath?
discovery.

the royalty for royalty.
how much for the use of hearts?
a musical ghost chanting

an invocation
an awakening

naima naima naima naima naima

all praise the muse
all praise the forgotten
all praise the goddess
all praise the wives.

marcia jessica asha dream tara latasha
liza leeza tamar-kali joi imani sonia nikky
sapphire alice keirna joan karen amina betty bell
veiled sisters

matriarchs of metaphor.
medusa un-stoned
dancing inside the moon.
how many lovers?
how many midnights?
howled. clapped.
mispronounced your name.
your exalted whisper.

Naima

blessed are those who trespass against you.

i want to see you. i want to see us.

face you
hear your smile

pull your heart from the mouth of his horn.

Blooooooooooooooooow.

make a wish.

tell
your
story.

haiku for Grace Lee Boggs

for her 97th birthday

she was born a girl.
first revolutionary
act. 1915

knew she was human
when goback was one word. pushed.
into herstory.

afro chinese black
power redefined her fire.
1963.

living is a threat
to the walking dead. grace smiles
jade eyes blink. one truth.

pre-riot love. grace
jimmy. workers for the pearl
between heaven and hell

her soundtrack?

the south. an umbilical cord
to the north. depending on what
you are try-n-ta birth. Ain't no new babies.
just new struggles.

these streets have names.
some of them are covered in blood
u can't just walk over our graves
without leaving a flower
for our blues. our city
has a name.

97 rebellions 970 love letters
9700 debates 97,000 more decades
97 million marches
tell me, what did you do with your life??

they listened to liberation music.

jazz was an original spirit. sometimes
the sound of an assembly line.
other times, a call to prayer
but it was always about transformation. always
a horn. a key to unlock humanity.

rebellion.

first there is a break. a crash.
then you must pick up the mirror.
hold it close to your face.
look deep inside your peace(s)
and build your revolution.

we hold our breath. grace.
as you did, while jimmy painted the garage.
our community, an extension of your exhale.

grace lee boggs
you are a helluva woman
inspiring a helluva lot of youth
impacting a helluva lot of future dreamers

to rebuild the city we inherited
through your courage and your fight

malcolm had betty
ossie had ruby
jimmy had so much grace.

transformationhaikus

for Malcolm X, always.

Detroit Red
Red clay greased down. pimp.
Mothers heart. the edge of freedom
Reborn a Little.

Hajj. Journey within.
Butterflies like Ali   fly.
This is my new name.

I found brotherhood
And now they want to kill me
Strange fruit. Same tree.   Falls.

My daughters survived.
Legacy hides in pigtails
Spirit combs through life.

Your smile made us smile.
Racism on their tongues. Hurt.
Joy don't break. Never.

Malcolm is a poem.
Blowing toward the east. Islam
Is a way of life.

Transformation time.
Focused despite threats. truth lives.
Change kissing your heart.

Wrap him in white silk.
Harlem man with Detroit walk.
Carry us home. With love.

You saw the bullet
& smiled. America breaks wide
                              open ocean.

I got my first death
Threat in nineteen ninety five
I was never scared.

I thought of you. Moved
To Brooklyn. Found Harlem. Home
Comings. Hand grenades. Detroit read.

As in
I read that book. My first band.
Inspired by your work.

There was a fire. In
Her belly. There was a fire.
Voice like water. Free.

My poems can't stop bul/
Lets. But bullets can't stop me
from writing more poems.

We took over schools.
Boycotted. Wore your X hats.
We sampled struggle.

Your blood still fresh on
The streets of New York. Detroit
We caught you. Mid-fall.

Shining prince. You gave
Us armor. Poets became
Poets in your light.

How many hands, huh?
To carry us home. Our grass
Roots. Moved 'cross 8 mile.

A long time ago.
50 years later. Your heart
beats. Sankofa style.

We don't cut the grass.
We still don't own the grass. We
still need you. Malcolm.

the **1979 bat**mobile

I was too busy worshipping my daddy
to take in every tear you swallowed.
I didn't fully process your long wait
at the bus stop in front of Michigan Bell
Phone Company.

You, armed with your 13th grade Canadian
diploma and four children to consider.
You weren't English or Canadian
anymore.

You were a Detroiter.
A British woman who could cook my
dear hunting daddy's deer and
a pot of collard greens like a
southern raised black woman.

It's 11:05 and we are up late in the middle
of summer negotiating who will sit in
the front seat.

I usually win. My little/taller sister would
kick the back of the passenger seat and
complain for the first few minutes of

our ride.

We were late this night. We usually came early.
Sat at the Tigers Restaurant
Downtown across from your job.

The house phone rang hard on 8059 Ward.
Your voice steady. A calm that made my daddy nervous.

That feminine silence that brews afternoon tea and cooks
Slow and purposeful meals.

Pressure cooker silence.

Your patient purse snatched off your arm.
Your stockings torn.
Knees scratched and cut from being pulled down.

She's okay, my daddy said, as we flew up
Michigan Avenue, past my future house
across from the old Tigers Stadium.

This purse snatching became my mother's liberation.

I don't think I noticed much about my mother when
my daddy was alive. At 10, I didn't know it was
strange that she didn't drive when my daddy's
convertibles came in colors.

A week later, the shiny bat mobile quietly and
courageously rolled into our driveway my daddy
poured with his own cement truck.

We. My brothers and my younger sister
who to this day
don't remember
because some memories stay missing when
you lose them.

Sometimes they come back when you
don't want them in anymore.

We were afraid.
Filled up with excitement.
She was planning it in secret.

Talking to my lanky yellow brothers.

Applying for the drivers license.

Finally standing up to our disciplinarian daddy
they loved and
feared.

The black Oldsmobile
We called the *Bat Mobile* was a
future get-a-way car
allowing my mother to simply drive
herself home from work

and one day

far, far away from

                    my daddy.

theyonlyaskaboutthehouse

i.

they only ask about the house.
the california king is on fire.
stolen soul pictures are wet.
dripping with blood and fear.
i cld only send so many back home.

there are cut outs of my last marriage on my mantel.
a mad house.
my home has turned into a circus.

there is a devil eating oreos and fried chicken
talking to her family on her phone
lounging on the third floor of my three
thousand square foot life.

i want to light a match. i love fire.
this wld be a great
exit.
king is so beautiful. so fragile.
my breasts were never sore when they had milk.

i felt so beautiful pregnant.
men wld ask me in public:
he's taking care of you mami?

yes. all 175 lbs and counting.

we are taking a vacation.
this. our first mother's day.
i invited evil into my home.

April 2007.
my son was just 8 months old.
the elder women wld shake their heads at me.
i was so naïve. too human for the jinn spirit.
i was off my square. i was nursing.
it was the happiest time of my life and
the devil was so jealous of
my smile. but i said, *yes*.

i allowed her, her kids, and
her nephew to come into our world
our personal space
and she went to work. inside out.

Garbage

is a place for evil to hide.
piles of garbage encased the place meant for
future big wheels, strollers, and car seats.

She wld leave pieces of her fake hair inside
brushes in my bathroom
dirty dishes in dresser drawers i
allowed her and her kids to use.
her kids slept in my stepson's bunk beds.

Single black female

hoping to be a matron of honor when
she was already   married.

no honor. in trusting women.
i worked hard to reverse this blasphemy.
played resurrection records in name of
the father, the son and

Jezebel?

Sade. Dianne Reeves.
Diana Reese. Angela Bofill
spirit is genderless.

Evil

doesn't
sing
this way.

ii.

i needed a bike in Georgia.
i was in another world.

Lost.

we are on the run
another night.
in our own southern city.

one escape
it was raining and some convention was in town
so we went to three different places.
Mommy wanted all
her breakdowns and getaways to be
stylish. free wireless.
gotta keep working.

yes. there is a poem in all of this.
sometimes you have to find words.
a beautiful man recently told me this.

Coarse.

this moment in my life was coarse.

iii.

i love men who use interesting words
flawlessly in a sentence
without hesitation or pre-meditation.
i know the type. they carry a small
trilingual dictionary in their pockets.
the word for today

Survival.

i am simply writing breaths.
i wonder how suicide is an
option for a mother. you kill your children 2.

i looked at king and wanted to live

two more lifetimes.
i've been here
7 years too long. on pause.
stroller jogger. too thin.

i cried when Kentucky Women's Writers Conference
sent me a letter asking me to perform the
Sonia Sanchez Keynote. i am not worthless after all.

iv.

pregnant poet with husband
attempting to kill me on the inside.
the digging is an excavation that helped
me find

Gold

enough to pack up my clothes.
he took the chaise out
our home. a gift from a holiday i
don't celebrate anyway.

king has his eyebrows. my dream child.
i ran so fast with you in my arms
too many times to count. running
from him. the man i love
changing into someone
i wld never recognize

again.

what about the house

?

they wld ask.

it can burn into the ground with
one thousand candles like
the end of Carrie!!!

i replied.

what about my womb?
the house that carried this joy.

v.

i remember people asking about my first husband when
i wasn't allowed to speak to my earth son.
i used to jokingly say he was in the closet.

brick is the only shelter

that will keep us safe. my daddy said:
never buy anything that's not brick.

i am brick and not for sale.

stucco skinned homes are so vulnerable so very
col/der sack temporary. mother's day. a sunday.
how convenient. we were at the W
or was it the Sheraton baby boy

?

vi.

we spent the day with the sun.
Centennial Park. Olympic Champions.
we are Twins. we are Braves.
we got Tiger Blood. we are Cherokee.

you have no idea that mommy is broken 100 times
in places with no finish line. no explanation for false
start when so pretty. no one will ever recognize this as
spring. everything is twisted.

i imagine us on horseback in Arizona.
you wrapped around the middle of my back.
a beautiful chief coming to our rescue.
my body, a rich reservation. taken over by
bandits. thieves
in my temple.

my geography will repair its wings and land.
fly backward
north for the summer.

write poems. start over.

give birth to you all over again.

After all
you were meant to be a
Detroit baby.

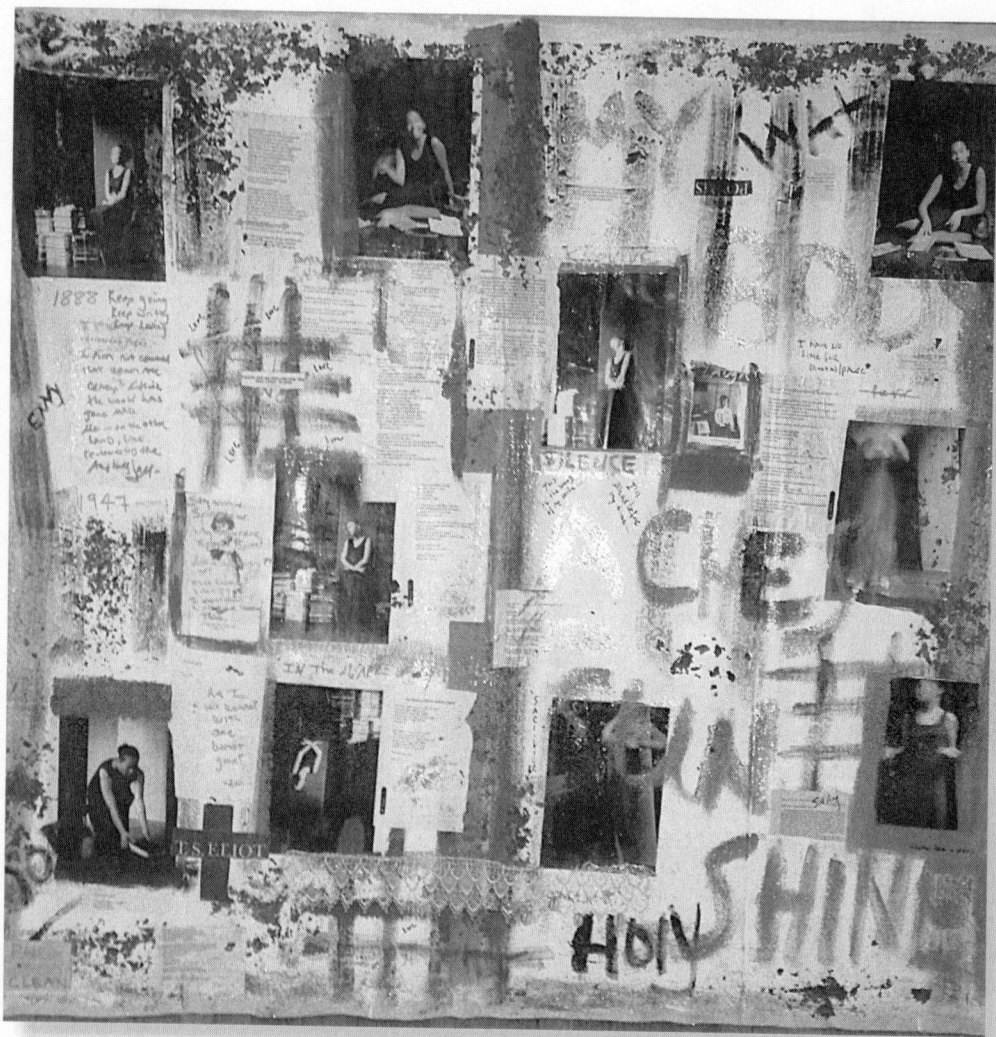

"No Asylums"
Vivienne Eliot
dried roses, rare photographs, poems,
acrylic on loose canvas, memories.

for**detroit,**in**honor**of**neighborhoods**day

If you've never slid down the GIANT SLIDE
on a potato sack then you may not know my
Detroit. If you've never eaten a Coney at 3 a.m.
you may not understand why
it doesn't matter how many games we win or lose
we wear our D HATS and tats year round.

Our streets were built to the rhythm of
a hand clap sound.
I am a Detroit Lion on Linwood
a rebellious Tiger on Tireman
a Stanley Cup carrying Red Wings on Rutherford.
a Detroit Piston constantly putting up new nets
Around forgotten white backboards and orange squares.

Rebellious cities never had it easy.
Innovative freeways aren't always paved in gold
but that thin strip of M-8 we call The Davison is a
conduit to every future highway in our nation
and so is the assembly line steel & wheels of our cars.

Detroiters always kept this country moving.

Revolutionary people don't always get good press
but it is in our DNA/ it is our bloodline gift
to survive.

When the surface of your skin has potholes
blasting Temptations' records through
your pores

When your fingertips are blessed
by international water and you are now
under the world's media microscope

constantly checking your arms for track marks
and close ups of how you look once the
high is gone

You are simply one city/ built above crystals
You are the river of freedom
You are the tenacity of Malcolm
The truth of Sojourner.
We are the fish fry at grannies
The Swim-Mobile
The Brightmoor Soccer Team
Dynamo's Deli on Plymouth
The Boggs Center
The Aker School For Gifted Children
The old school sweet of Dutch Girl Donuts
and the Sweet Potato Sensation cakes across the street
from the mural covered beauty we call Artist Village.

We exist in the brilliance of our young debaters
Our champion athletes our self empowered rockers
Our young farmers/ and dancers and scientists and
Future social activists.

We are 5 E Gallery and Arise Detroit and
Black WOMEN Rock! We are N'namdi Gallery and
The Charles H. Wright and Goodwell's and the opposite of
white flight.

Our babies are Ice Dreamers.
Young souls on ice.
Hockey players up early
at Butzel on Wyoming and Lyndon.
We are cultivating young visual artists
at Cultural Roots Art Camp
inside Mama Makini's home every summer on Prentis.

We are Coach Shaheed's Basketball Camp at Renaissance
We are all necessary coaches who act as fathers and
moms who create safe sanctuaries and
Rite of passage programs for our daughters
beautiful Detroit sistas.

We are not urban fiction.

When the pulse of our city stops beating
the soul of american music and manmade industry dies
a metropolis with a broken heart
a split in half baseball field for months
a train station with broken stained glass eyes
that can still reflect we are a city with pride
our neighborhoods fighting for their namesake.

We may have abandoned homes but we
are not an abandoned people.
I hear outsiders talking about a New Detroit
but I remember the beauty of Old Detroit.

Block parties/the Cass Co-op/and
late night car races.
Hip Hop Shop and 7 smile strip

Tigers baseball around a bonfire on any corner played
 loud enough for the entire block to listen.

I was raised inside this sound.

I walked down Joy Road to get to school.
I found lifelong friends on Ward Street/Stahelin
Pinehurst/Mendota/Manor/Littlefield
Tireman/Plymouth/West Chicago/Rosedale Park
Mack and Bewick/Gratiot/Harper/Conner
Cadieux/Mansfield/French Road/Heidelberg

Jefferson/Van Dyke/St Aubin
Bagley/Porter/Church/Holbrook/Evergreen
Vernor/Marston/North End/Livernois
Chandler Park/Rouge Park/Palmer Park

I was raised on
Hamilton Bus Stop stories
The Purple Gang glory
Hudson's and Kresge's Five and Ten
When Belle Isle was open and live
way past ten.

We the spirit rising inside Alice Coltrane's holy ghost harp
We the *ooh baby baby* that made Smokey's smile melt tears
We the Wonder Bread smell of Stevie's harmonica
An international legend making city.
We are used to stones being thrown against our glassy lakes.
Detroiters don't do fake.
We do work. We make art. Out of our neighborhoods
We made Anita Baker/ Mike Banks/Juan Atkins/and Derrick May.
We made the Queen of Soul/ and John Doe.
We made Proof and Slum Village/and white M & M's
We made Jackie Wilson/ David Ruffin
The Supremes and Winans.

We make characters like Dreadlock Mike and
Willie Jenkins who told me:

We made jump rope from wire
We used to make everything.

We birthed two of the Fab Five and claim the whole team
We the Bad Boys and the Errol Flynn.
Don't talk about a city's feet
when these are shoes you can't fit in.

We don't sleep in late.
We don't wait for someone else to do it.
We surrounded by masters.
We the graves they love to walk over.
We the people the census don't always count correctly.
We are the sum of our grandmothers prayers
and our Native ancestors' wishes.

My brothers had to take out the garbage.
I busted suds in the kitchen.
We southern rooted. Country.
Alabama/Mississippi/and Georgia.
We grassroots soldiers.
We Damon's Records and Spectacles on Grand River
We the after-hours.
Concrete and Flowers
We know peace and
Joe Louis black power.

We the blue collar inside the rainbow of humanity.

We the assembly line of work ethic and
Union muscle.
Jays Chips and Faygo Red hustle

We are EASTERN MARKET ON SATURDAYS

We a city of of Masjids/Synagogues/Temples
And Baptist Church preachers
We fly hijab/wrapped sisters on Friday/and some of the finest
Church suit brothas you'll ever see on any given Sunday.
Muhammad Mosque Number 1/Fellowship Chapel
Greater Grace/ Hartford Memorial/ and We Triumph.
We Bakers Keyboard Lounge and the legacy of Berts.

Some of us young enough to know that there is

young genius being brewed in this city
in the keys of Jon Dixon/in the trumpet of Kris Johnson
in the writing of dream hampton/inside the sax of Ladarrel and
De'sean/the voice of Steffanie Christi'an/Thornetta Davis/ and Monica Blaire.
We Dwele and Miz Korona/Black Milk/Wajeed, Invincible & Ideeyah
We DJ Dez/ Hot Waxx/Sacari/and One Belo
We are Khalid's *Center of the Movement.*

Detroit has spirits. Not just the statue in front of the
Coleman A. Young Building.
We got real time spirits and Ancestor spirits.
All of them protect our city. Stand as guardians.
Our historians have names/ buy coffee at Avalon
Still eat Coney dogs at Lafayette
Drink Detroit Red
Go to Sweetwater for the wings
Enjoy the dark lights at Union Street
Value the Cass Café.

Detroit is easily translated into
French and South African Apartheid and
The Berlin Wall crumbling down
Jewish and African holocausts
Black men in Italian suits
Shades painting live at the Torino Music Festival
And Underground Railroads Stops.

Stop

and find a major city in this country
find a musician on this planet that
doesn't Respect Our History.

MLK didn't preach his dream here first for no reason.

Woodward avenue is the spine of movements.
Michigan Avenue baseball left arm pitching.
Grand Boulevard right leg walking.
The steel and grind of Techno still breathing just
east of Downtown.
We wipe away the tears of clowns.
America would not be America if not
for the Motown sound.

The integrity and heart of our people are not bankrupt.
We are rich with history. Raised on tradition
Our Daddy's lessons and our Momma's intuition.

We have coaches and teachers and parents
And activists and leaders on the frontline
Of this river/front.
We ride bikes down the Dequindre Cut.
Maybe you've heard of us.

We the people inside the Michigan hand
Indigenous Detroiters and we love our land
We make artists with international fans
I'm from a Detroit hood
So I'm a part of the plan
Somebody gotta show the young ones
How to get up 75
We not ghosts riding.
We live and work in this city and

We Are Alive.

Temporary Shelter

i catch the rain

calculating the ocean
dropping. the sky falling
safely into a strangers
world.

have i gone mad
?
i'm so mad he's gone
which one?
i wasn't here when
                    he left.

i want him to come home
to a place i've named
temporary shelter.
a place to heal & move.

this earth keeps pulling me
back down into this place
where i've buried my
wounded heart countless times.

this land of broken promises.
this nation of liars.
i will not give birth
surrounded by all this fear.
dilated history. how many lessons?

my patience is thin. i know i'm a
queen. i don't have to place it
inside my name.
i carry those ancient women in
the marrow of my bones.

no longer in love
with this cold. i eat the snow.

i suppose/i'm supposed to feel old.
but i am watching my son begin.
so i begin again.

with my world emptied out by
sadness & lost

in my city.

bloodshed is in the waterfalls.
the cliffs on every corner.
death breathing inside the wind
watching my steps/i miss walking
for miles.

so why not love   now?

when there is nothing left
i don't know how to be subtle.
i know i am balance. light.
weightless & beautiful
in your hands.

i write haiku as prayer.
give them to you in small
pieces. every bead a sound
every reach for the sun
another poem
pulled from your smiling
face.

my cherokee blood split
by arrows/dipped in tar

blessed by frankincense
chewed & spit out
for protection.

i just want a safe place.
just wish for freedom that
doesn't require me to scream
freedom.

eventually i will grow numb
from complacency.
gypsy woman must head
east. again.

i want to be still. i want
to marry stillness. over & over
again.

want to place it on my tongue

& sleep off these sleepless
nights. i cry for days.
i've loved men my whole life.
my daddy was first.

the doctrine of brown girls.
the hearers of the new news.
we are old friends. fast.
we the holders of time
translating sankrit on sacred skin
whispering our children's names.
stars. clearing the clouds.

i want to laugh aloud
for a million more years
measure my losses in kilometers.

inches away from being blind
i can see your scars.
tell your brothas on mars.
thank you.
tell mother earth. we love her.
honor the present.
abandon fear. dance with wolves.
wear the silver tie. wear the coffee.
the lemon. the blue. the subtle bling.

i'll wear my feathers.
i'll tattoo it to my yellow Thailand spine.
i'll pretend to drink wine & wear
matching heels. i'll wear my jesus
sandals & meditate
with you. touch knees. hold hands.

my red afro a humble satellite.
a crown of tangled flowers
seasoning Detroit curry.
i call possibility   truth.

how is it possible to feel?
how it it possible not to feel?

when i feel everything.

my dream catcher is blue

cowrie shells. glowing.
sometimes crying. a native
woman. mourning. it's 11:43 p.m.
you have already passed another
morning. i will never catch up
in this world of backward clocks.

i burn the midnight oil with
arabian sandalwood & mango
tea on my lips.

i know you are in the sun.
moon. child.

i simply

catch the rain.

jessica in summer

for R.S. (thank you)

The roses are dipped in graffiti
The bananas are Josephine's
Gil Scott Heron showed up in our Detroit
Tribute as an Ancestral bird
Sankofa Pigeon

&

I was kissed by rock & roll
Right in the mouth.

I've been singing this music
since Motown pigtails wailed
in the mirror/concertos coupled with
hair brush in the shower microphones
giving the holy ghost to little brown girls
segregating their hearts from their bodies
too early.

To damn young to know all them love songs
since reading Janis Joplin's autobiography
& thinking Lorraine Hansberry was the
most beautiful lady with black eyes
on the cover of a paperback book.

I knew this music was mine.
The electricity of guitar's sensitive teeth biting
my not quite grown up lips
waiting for *this* sound to
one day kiss me back.

& it did.

In the middle of a crowded
airport in the city of wind
before the refrain
had a chance to find itself
in the middle of a Hendrix howl
before reminding you

I am clear how i entered

this planet. So how I exit the
weekend/the moon/tour bus
mother ship/stage

don't matter baby.

I was born with stardust poems
& magic bones walking
inside stories of the children
of Bahia while drinking tears
I've swallowed whole in a torrential
apartheid rain in the heart of Soweto.

Tears.

I am fearless in this skin.

I have felt the pain of hundreds of
Little girls inside a fanatic hug/shake
& cry in my arms/in the name of poems
they claim saved their lives.

I know that fame is a lie.

You/wrapped around my tired
single mom-full time-artist body from
Chicago to Minneapolis & back

was the beautiful/quiet melody
of this moment.
Maybe I just needed to sleep
inside this music. wheels against
concrete. rollin.

Stillness while moving.

The palm of your hand
holding onto a fantastic wood wallet.
I forget to ignore the obvious.

You somebody too?
The waiter asks.

Well, aren't we all?

Talking about golf/childhood teachers
with you telling me what I
already know
    'bout me.

I love like a southern woman.

In my head I am thinking of
recipes to feed you in an imaginary
kitchen.

This is what women do
to figure out if they love a song.
They play it loud while cooking.

Can't count the thousands of
times I've said goodbye to
music. Turned off the radio
out of boredom with meaningless lyrics.

Sometimes the song stays in your head
for several days in a row. Even if
you don't like it. If it's real
good/it never truly leaves
your body. Some women
die with an 8 bar blues buried
inside their womb.

This summer her music is alive.
Breathing through the untold truth of
Betty Davis. Alive as Coltrane's
inspirational & indefinable Naima.

This ain't the first time some giving music
kissed a giving poet in the mouth.

They always had compatible mouths.

This ain't the first time she's played
a record this authentic. She's been rolling
to this soft needle/black orpheus soundtrack
laying softly against the round black

ever since.

Nothing like a man who takes all your things out of some other mans
hands and says: "That's alright man, I got all of that."

complicated beyond the math

for coach

I'm complicated beyond the math
I'm too old to wear a mask. I'm
Too pretty to have to ask.

I'm so simple & shy with you.
I have all the answers. Yes.
Two plus two.

I've divided my days. I want to fit
It all in. life is so short & I know
magic is thin.

you understand   the unsaid.
That's why I still   need to write it.

I need your breath.
I need your wondrous hands/your deep voice
Your wolf growl/your bear/your bits of silver hair
Your heavy heart/your light/laugh/unbroken smile

I need someone to push me off the track.
This train traveling at the speed of light.

Slow down

Starfish. Surrounded by so many wounded capes
claiming to save you from
your next fall from grace.

Be still

I know you can see too much too fast.
It's the curse of the past/ the gift is
tomorrow. I am not the sum of my sorrow.
We are not the sum of our sorrows.
Something blue. Something borrowed.

Sun swallowed. Clouds for hair.
Earth as skirt.

Here's your lunch baby.
Love to watch you work.

I wonder

When they excavate my work like
Dickinson when I'm deep in the dirt.
When they deconstruct the lines.

Will they
Find your voice. Your black gold oil.
You are
a river of stories between my bones.
Desert children. Our winter home.
Your approach is water.

Invisible.

I am a woman in my deepest tone.
I am light. I am home.
Fear of happiness keeps us all alone.

We born crying for hope. We die before dying.

I just want a quiet place.
A simple piece of real estate.
Move inside an outlet along your
ocean hands & plug my electric
drum
          heart in.

We Are
Not Ghosts

Sunlight Through Bullet Holes

jessica falling from the sky

after Jimmy Santiago Baca

I am jessica falling from the sky
8 bar blues falling from the moon
I am blue glass cutting thru clouds
I was born on purpose.
Native and loud.
I am drinking from this southern well
I've learned to land in the best of hell
Can't you see me walking by?

I am jessica falling from the sky
I am jessica falling from the sky

I am landing and I can't lie.

I am not a ghost. My memories are the future
In reverse. I cannot be this lie. Not again. Paraded
As fools, we, beautiful women. Believe the parrot.
On repeat. We hear what we want to hear.

When they cut off my ear, I grew an extra eye.
Green-blue diamond. Pupil. Open. Never stone.
He promised. I'm coming with you. This whisper
Replaced my right lobe and kept me all these years.

Enough that he showed up. It didn't matter
What time. How late. Which century.
No tongue is foreign
When in   love.

We speak universal. We memorized our mouths.
Even when taped shut, the truth always escaped.
Chomsky kissed
A poet.

These are my eyes. All three of them.
Five, counting your two.
I still couldn't see far back enough,
To anticipate the outcome

How high the river would rise
How simple magic would be mislabeled witchcraft
How I would run out of words and feel death traveling
In full sentences.

I am young skin surrounded by aged sounds
& patch/work patterns of music. Dancing in time.
Drowning in beautiful illusions.

Honesty is breath without trying.
Strangers are mythological creatures.
I miss you without trying.
We've just met.
I've known you my entire past life.

I'm not excusing my present behavior.
Angels know it's difficult to pretend to not
Smell light & sleep when u are awake.
Women do this their entire lives. It wasn't
Until I closed up the sun between my legs
That some real light could shine through.

He came with good intention.
Mistaken identity. Maybe.
I don't question the right now.
We artists. So we live in it.
I got caught off guard against
My 1989 silver Volvo.

We don't get many hot nights

In this part the country. What
Was I supposed to do, drive off?

I couldn't move.

I couldn't even feel a real kiss
Until deep into the summer of
His mouth. You know the kind.
Where you get lost in it for several minutes.

That was the beginning of my freedom
Weekend. I simply said yes to the universe
for the first time in centuries.
I'd been talking about men
In their shoes for 730 days.

I wouldn't even look in their faces
when they said, hello. Just the shoes.
How a man stands next to the spirit of a
woman. So many. of us. forced.
into silence
in the interest of ego
& maintaining a household

My friend told me I needed to recognize
The beauty of my alien-like qualities.
Long yellow block your shot arms.
Poet's heart.
Daddy's loaded rifles.
Sanchez razor blade teeth
& tongue warm & body lined with
A century old fire
Burnt orange
Wild seed. Mis-planted.

Purity is not rewarded
Poems are not for sale
Pussy is born free
Dick is not always the key
To life but it makes life
More interesting.

I learned that the second time
I fell from the sky.

I am jessica falling from the sky
8 bar blues falling from the moon
I am blue glass cutting thru clouds
I was born on purpose.
Native and loud.
I am drinking from this southern well
I've learned to land in the best of hell

Can't you see me walking by?
I am jessica falling from the sky
I am jessica falling from the sky

call our names

words run into each other the way
strangers often do. ancestors reflect
in faces. pretty poems don't always
come from pretty places.

i am zora in search of the anthropology
of my beginning. i am no one's secret.
every chapter/every syllable released
an undefinable billie. set free
chasing after love between
breaths and battles with mediocrity
the space love demands. surrounded
by the comfort of band. stage.

we watch the heart beat of tones
move with the sound of voice.

i was headed to the sun and found the moon.
i was racing to the sun and landed   here.

hearts don't lie. history does. the faceless
profound naima/the pride of abbey. watch
her land. all fours. how many doors. back
to where we make art. life.

others allow you to assume
they are happy off the stage
our lungs and legs as maze.
a beautiful mess.

sometimes our spirits just josephine.

misbehave.

take that freedom to your grave.
the doctrine of the honest liar.
workers for the paper world
native by numbers. paint by colors
my palms still wet with rich mud

and the promise of love. i simply
want moor. somebody stole a moor.
we want peace on our earth's
floor boards
tangled noosed mic cords.

blues bit my bottom lip and laughed
put it on my epitaph:

she was a poet.

i see langston. in harlem.
i hear sara and supremes
brewing black tea in a detroit project
low rise. we rise. between
heavy breaths and shots of rum
ginger spiced tongues and red
clay suited alabama blues
men. playing cards in gangsta
alligator church
shoes. traveling. moonlight to mark
the corner magic of our journey.

survival. a map scarred/face.
a path along my spine. a treasure
chest carved along my rib cage.
where are the fruits of my labor
pushed and sold
how many mothers have i been
how many babies have i lost

how many hearts
seven? i hold them like dimes
in an invisible pocket my daddy
stitched to my skin.

like morning stillness
the brief quiet before the volcano bleeds
which ear shld i wear my petals

?

Sing till the ugly turns bright
for you.
lilacs dipped in rouge

upside down rainbows.
we slide easily into this emancipated
language. me always running from

me.

i am searching for the sound
hidden behind the music.
frida's monkey on my shoulder
meditating.

i'm asking for God's forgiveness
for taking so long to acknowledge
the circle. for standing on the other side
of it as it moves. waiting for my turn
to jump in. double dutch.

i've learned

joy is obtainable several days in a row.
welcome to the glory of the uninvited

the doctrine of the clairvoyant
the beauty of the authentic
the politics of the reviewer
the need to be never be understood
is all i'll ever need from outsiders.

it is difficult to explain ourselves.

the black voice is eaten
but never deconstructed at the table.
i'm eating poems today
i'm running with wolves
making love to magnolia trees
firing at the limitless sky.

how much light is allowed
on this planet. thank God we
always turning. don't nobody
wanna see that much truth
standing still. i hit the keys
like piano. i swallow horns
and drink strings like water.

u got your hand on the throat

the pulse of my greatest discovery.

breath.

the shit we do without thinking.
this is what makes us flawless
this is what makes us genius.
call our names.

in the dark hour of someone else's
daytime diary. i'm crying inside the

irony. had to learn to love the fire in me.

call our names

betty
miles
john
nina
etta
duke

inside the metaphor for madness
in the jazz mouth of your fingers
in the fascination of perception
in the past life lover resurrection
in the dream state of the dreamers
in the owl's glance. on the ocean floor
i hear   dawn breaking.
cracking open. like the boogie down
like the A train on Sunday
waiting. always waiting for the teacher
to simply
call our names
call our names

so we can tell our stories
so we can serve the music
wash this mystery off our skin
carve it into the stomach of our
curved bark. our cherry wood tongues
paper for the ink-less.

we write it in the air
                we scream in the clarity of the blurry
in the flame of the banned book.
the same road we followed east

is the same street we were born.
my feet have traveled every inch of
this earth. Fearlessly.
birth is no different than death in me.
it's the definition of change.

call our names
in the back of your throats
in the illusion of the educated
in the hypocrisy of the holy
in the steal of the night
it always comes to light.
a whisper always finds the scream
a memory always finds a home.

call our names
so we can find the others
and warn them. About love.
before the evitable fall.
the invisible line returning them
to the edge.

where it all began
and where it will always

      end

there was a fire in her belly

there was a fire in her belly

1971.
Tom and Irene answered back.
Made their
First post-riot daughter.
Bottle-fed naivety and rainbows
That included black.
And pride.
1971.

She questioned everything

There was a fire in her belly.
Uh huh
There was a fire.
But can't nobody afford no fires
In Detroit.
She betta give that baby back.

I could hear the gun shots
Mixed with Isaac Hayes.
My brothers pretending to
Know karate, blue brown
Belts, chopping the wind.
I knew I was different early.
I used to like to break glass
And examine the mirror.
For hours at a time.

I knew I was somebody's secret
I didn't start all them fires.
I'm just little girl.
I'm just little brown girl.
I'm just pigtails and poems in waiting.
The words just came out that way.

Twisted. Transformed into something
New.
Something I could eat and not choke on.

This was my story and I was gonna tell it.
Whether they wanted me to or not.

I was nine when I attempted to write my first novel.
I don't know if I'd read nine novels, but I was
Nine and I wanted to write one.

Still writing it. Still writing it.

They say there are ghosts in that house I was
Born in. Running up and down the stairs.
Maybe they looking for the family that used
To fill it up. Checking for the pencil markings
On the walls to score how tall we'd grown
And the bird that died and the dogs that ran
Off sometimes.

Maybe they are just looking for the kids.
Four to a house minimum
Used to make this block noisy.

Maybe they are trying to find at least one two family
Household in this city.

They could just be bored.
Might be laid off. Stressed out.
Sometimes ghosts take to running.

I know I did. For 12 years I was gone.
Like the wind. Ghost! But the wind just moves
In circles. Smoke signals.
They say. Picking up dust and a husband or

Two. Least I'm trying. Least I'm writing.
Somebody gotta tell 'em

We

are

not

ghosts.

In 2010
4,828 young people ages 10 to 24
were victims of homicide—an average of 13 each day.

love is about the math
for JK

How much time you spend with someone
divided by everything else
you have to do

to live.

drink water. eat. breathe. laugh. pee. shit. sleep.

X > breathing = love

Love is about the math.

In 8th grade I negotiated my way out
of trigonometry. I told my principal:
I'm going to Michigan State
to be a writer and I won't need math.

It was ruining my grade point average.
& threatening my future life
happiness at 17.

During my 4 years at Cody High School
We experienced one of the worst school
related shootings in history.

I feel as if this statistic is said after every
school shooting to follow. It's like the leading epidemic
for blk anything was always about 15 different diseases
and of course, homicide.

I don't know how pain. death. loss. betrayal and tears
found their way into this perfect equation.

Life is about problem solving. Memorizing the formula.

Light divided by Death

An average speeding bullet may travel
1,000 feet per second.
from your basic 22 caliber hand gun.

Sunlight takes about 8.3 minutes to reach the Earth.

Eight thousand three hundred feet of flying death
to reach the vulnerable surface of

Skin.

The leathery husk of a man. The hairy rind of stories
Tattooed on the arms of boys.

I need to figure out this
                    new math.

Love is not a rational equation when murder
is the common. denominator.

The amount of time it takes before sunlight
can find its way through earth/skin's surface.

How much time before
                    joy & light return.

How many losses? How many pints of blood?
How many bodies can one mother hold?

On average, it takes energy between
10,000 and 170,000 years
to leave the sun's interior and
be emitted from the surface as

light.

I can't wait that long for us to move.

For change.

There are other factors.
Weight of gun powder. Type of Gun.
Atmospheric conditions.

How articulate is she on the stand?
How low are his pants off his ass?

What are his SAT scores?
Where is his daddy?
What color was the hoodie? How large the nose?
How African the arms. How Native his cheeks.
How Ogun his spirit?

Does the bullet ever consider how deeply it will
Destroy the fabric/the family's peeled back skin

?

Velocity of a 50 caliber bullet varies.
Barrel length. Bullet weight. Powder charge.
Minus the velocity of a 15 year old boy in St. Louis
Who can't make it home without his piece.

Length of legs: 4.5 ft. Weight: 125. Power: unrealized.

We. Sun children. We. Limbs of steel street lights.
We are the corner gossip.
The story the bullet will never know.
The warms nights that steal our babies voices.

Like taking candy from a baby

Skittles Now & Laters.
Our Stars/burst
Shot through the heart.
We give love/a bad name.

We. the broken circle. We. the silent blast.
A black hole.
We inhale haiku in one breath.
Push out peace.

Long live Radio Rahim!
His Love Verses Hate
Do The Right Thing Fists
Monologue our post racial fingers.

infinity times infinity.

I need a equation that cures broken hearts
Subtracts loss. I need some new
Number 2 pencils. Some lead

you can't erase. Love engraved in
permanent ink.

drink water. eat. breathe. laugh. pee. shit. sleep (repeat)

I was born a hunter. I know some men prefer to be
the predator but my daddy was a
deer hunter. The innocence of young boys are
alive in the eyes of a fawn.

I can still see blood on his trigger finger.
Words become light on my tongue.

Sometimes we are forced to swallow & cook
& eat this pain

infinity

times

infinity

dear **meat**

I no longer eat you.
My daddy was born in Madison, Alabama.
His rifles hung in the garage
indifferent & skinny as my 7 year old legs
flying past most boys on the block.

I cld never take the rich scent of venison.

My mother swears to this day she
never cooked any of that stuff.
Chittlins, deer meat, coon.
I remember that funk filling up our kitchen
& I never saw my daddy doing anything
'cept eating or preparing his homemade bar-b-q sauce
during our family cook outs on Ward street.

My brothers knew I loved animals.
I wld cry when they shot
squirrels or birds with their b b guns.
My daddy's guns were different.

I never saw him kill a fawn.
Only witnessed the limp body falling from
the top of his car.

Mark and Johnny would terrorize me.
Chase me with furry hooves.

Raising my son vegetarian was my long awaited apology.

He will never wish you dead or prepare
you as a meal as his namesake
reloads his rifle &
waits

to teach the grandson he never met
how to hunt in the

afterlife

Love,
King's Mom

bullet points for the **reader**

for the Mausi family

Bullets that strike a target at an extreme angle
will usually leave an elongated hole.
These holes typically will still have fairly even margins.
Almost all non-contact bullet entrance holes will be smaller in
diameter than the bullet due to the elasticity of the fabric.

Hassan Sundiata Malik Green was in a wheelchair.
Wheels angled east. Murdered in Detroit.

Feburary 15th 2011.

Some of us born with prayer beads
& not enough time in our mouths.

He danced for Nelson Mandela
3 months after he was released from prison

& came to Detroit to speak.

He wore an African inspired fabric.
Holes only where the arms go.

He always looked as if he was elevating
when he danced.

Hasaan and his partner Kafani.

We knew him as Theo.
Before he moved to Senegal and saw his reflection

In all those faces. Didn't come home for a decade.
I've loved so many ocean eyed men

born with hip hop legs and elastic wings.

In Detroit, Ramadan is always coming.
His daughter and son are the even margin.

The non contact entrance hole.
Malika is 11 and wears his full smile and
watery bright hazel eyes.

At which angle does the bullet see the target
& everyone that dies in the diameter of the

doorway of the dramatic exit

?

Stylish bullet. Dressed for death. Jacketed.
Leaving residue rings. Lead primer.

Holes passing through the fragile
ripped material of men.

Men of steel & rubber & Motor City Muscle

Yale
Proof
Hassan
John Doe
Terry Dwyer
Batin

Midwest sky at half mask
Allah in their hearts.

Smiling is
a revolutionary act
                in this city.

there has to be a safe place for boys

for Trayvon Martin & my sons King, Omari, Jaden & Israel
And Shaima Alawadi

there has to be a safe place for boys
brown boys who lace their will & dreams
inside designer shoes
Untraceable boys we lose with no media attention
to the prison industrial complex.

we. complex. beautiful. boys.

rocking headphones to block out the reality
sometimes it takes a head nob so u can truly see
the God in me.

i know
they walk at night like stars
cuz they created this astrology
so when one of ours is taken
we want justice
not apologies

i wanna walk in a store
or from a store
with no one trying to follow me.

you follow me?

We birth our babies unarmed. A war
being raged against their existence
at conception.

brilliant young Kings in the making.
searching for footing on a rich soil.

wet cement pulling them back into
america's schizophrenic quick sand.

this land with their veins deeply rooted
inside southern trees with stories passed
down thru hands covered in white cotton and
sugar red dyed skittles in their pockets
we die
too easily

for a whistle
or a glance
driving while black
breathing
how do we protect them from the decay of history
institutionalized racism. segregated
privatized classrooms.

Mama Kadiatou Diallo's blood in these oceans
Mama Amina Baraka's daughter's heart
in their teeth

our city just lost

Hassan Mausi Green
Njoma Yale Miller

Five children in San Diego just lost their mom
Shaima Alawadi
because of her choice to wear a
hijab

countless others…

We swallow violence whole after pushing
our potential beauty into this world.

the least we cld offer our children

is safety.

We are simply mothers running with our sons
away from bullets. from the poverty of
mis-education.

Our twilight children. Black gold survivors
we melt down and mold into men.
We the forgotten holocaust
the genocidal genuflecting
cross we bare—
On your knees
hands behind your back.

Our neighborhood watch
created the heavens.

who are you to play God?

i watch black boys' free spirits at 5 turn to dust
by 13 in these streets.

it is difficult to walk upright
when you know a wrong move
can kill you.
hands in your pockets is a
death sentence.
running can get you killed.
dancing is illegal and
simply standing on a corner
with your friends is lethal.

they suck the cool out of black boys to
sell their cars and shoes

then criminalize them for looking like
their own ad campaign

a brotha in a hoodie or saggy jeans has never
treated me any worse than a suit and tie noose

Trayvon Martin is all of our sons.
hoodie up and jeans low.
Ogun spirit. sometimes misdirected
anger. when has this country pointed
a gun in the right direction?

the war against our sons and daughters is unspoken
yet always present. the tanks are invisible here.
sometimes violence is in the water.

it becomes a part of our lives. what we drink.

We. the children of movements.
We were not meant to be still.
We extensions of the earth.
We the future fathers of time.
We the ones they couldn't kill.
We the chosen. We the excellent athlete.
The power suit. The feared.
The pilot. The educators. Our boys

targeted while attempting to outlive their circumstance
to walk in a place that detached legs from
trees that bore strange fruit and gave birth to blues.

are we to push them back up into our wombs
to save them from a life of inhumanity?
where is the sonia sanchez haikued
vision of peace?

we raise our daughters and pray for our sons.
just make it home from school.

sanford. ramallah. joy road. brooklyn. detroit. chicago.

i see Trayvon in my son's face every morning.
Sybrina Fulton is mourning.

there has to be a city. a planet. a neighborhood.
a block a village a farm a solar system
a safe place for   boys
a safe place for girls

born with the massai. lean legs. deep brown eyes.
cherokee cheekbones.
the son our president never had

another displaced flag in his 17-year old body
by a stranger claiming a discovery/a victory
over   something
you can never discover/or win
when your peace

is loaded in your piece.

the beautiful intangible geography of a black boys life
is difficult to navigate in the narrow slanted view of
american racism.

Trayvon Martin
refusing to run.
in the aftershock of a post-racial lie.

We will stand our ground.
We will shake the earth like Shango

awaken mothers who haven't slept since the 1400's
in this country
anyway.

We will align ourselves with humanity.
you can't keep killing us randomly

in the name of Malcolm, Martin, Emmitt
Betty, Coretta, Harriet, Merlie, mothers.

Trayvon Martin
will pilot the change
Trayvon
soaring beyond his 17 year old years
Trayvon
is the defiant wind passing thru

we must relocate our leaders
inside five year old warriors.
hide pens and truth inside pigtails
so the struggle

is always made new.

March 26 2012
Read during Detroit's Hart Plaza rally for Trayvon Martin.
By invitation from Donnell White, NAACP Executive Director
and Kevin Tolbert, UAW Assistant Director

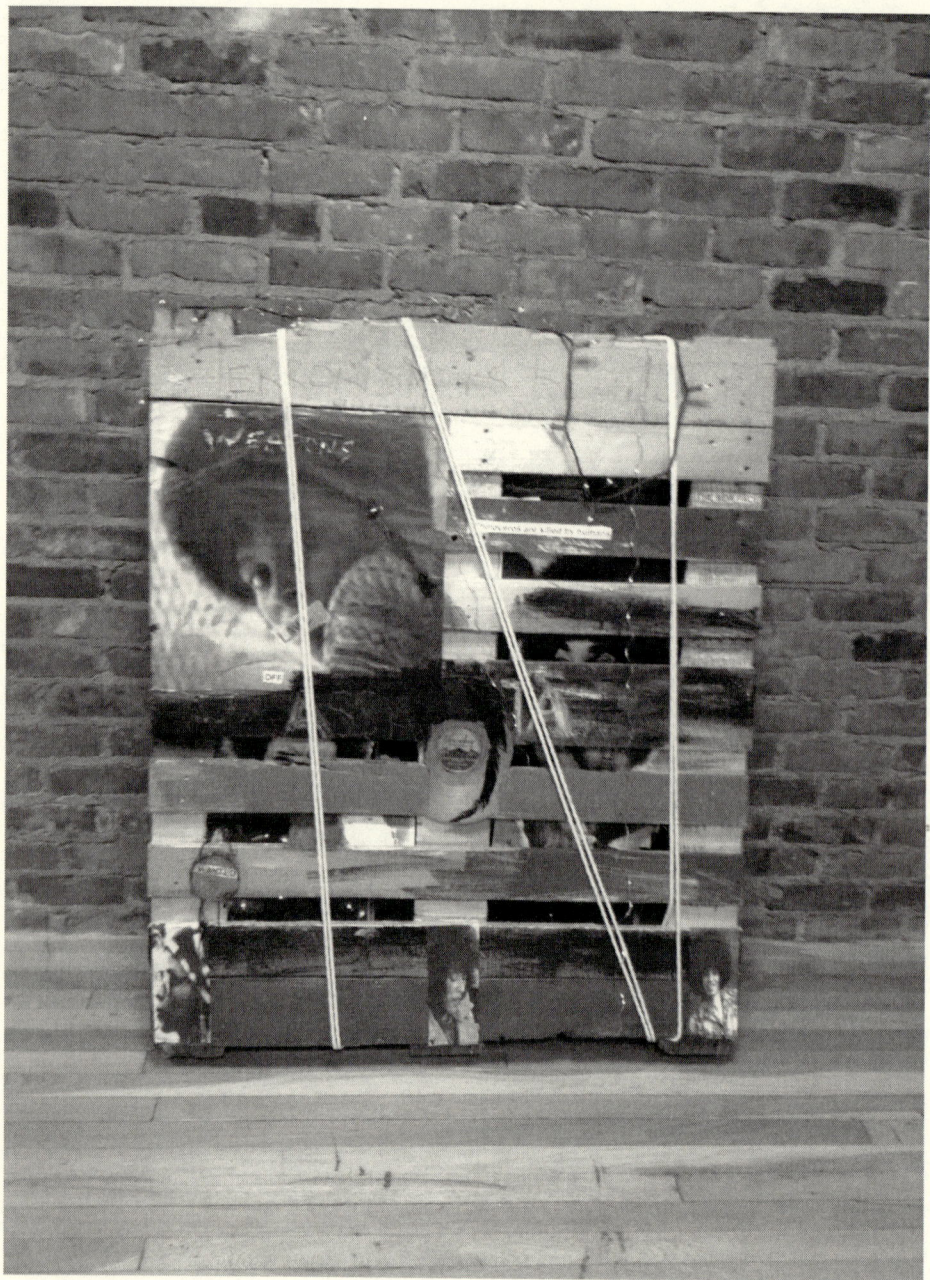

"Terrorism is beautiful"
Found wood, acrylic, photos, painted live

for **joann watson**

when a brown girl child is born
the earth shifts, the sun is at half mask
the moon waits for the first cry.

the ancestors set the table
the flowers turn red as blood
this is your land, continent daughter with
tree trunked legs & branches for
arms.

this is your soil, black and fertile
as your eyes facing an apartheid jim crow
current past memory.

some of us begin the removal of shackles at birth
we grow into the armor of struggle quickly.
we brew courage in our tea
blend bravery into our sunday dinners
we find our voice & we use it to speak for many.
we find our power & put it in the hands of the youth
we see the injustices. the imbalance of nature & wealth

Joann Watson, you understand that nation building is not
a part time job. this work is a long walk
this dedicated life is sometimes a lonely, vulnerable choice
but it is the only way you
know how to operate.
you are wired for the movement. in your black women bones
even when tired, still fighting, still organizing.

still singing morning spirituals

you were born to lead, even in your own family
the eldest of 10 children born to Jefferson & Lestine Nichols.

Damon, Nefertari, Stephen, Maya—
her children always knew she was larger than life.

when you are a woman in the movement
you take the children with you on the journey
you bring your babies with you to your college classes.
when you travel to Ghana for the first time, it will be
with daughters in tow.

when you are a fearless nationalist thinking momma
mothering never stops with your own babies—
thirty god children and mentees across the country.

the daughter of a ministering mother is already ordained
for good trouble.
a see-er. a prophetic young student.
preparing for her lifelong role as

servant to her own community.

when u suddenly became a single mom, people told you
what you couldn't do. instead you moved to NYC with all four
of your seeds to do your necessary work with the YWCA.

Queens make it look easy.

When your purse was stolen at a Farmer Jacks
with your children's tickets to Run DMC inside
you found a way to get your babies into the concert and
hosted *Melle Melle* and the *Furious Five* in your living room.

Queens make it look easy.

Ghana....Togo....South Africa

where is your heart Mama Watson

?

nurturing spirit. baking melt in your mouth
homemade biscuits.
how many hours do you sleep Warrior Watson?
with endless work ethic and blue collar blood
racing through your veins?

how do we say *thank you* for your work
your time, your heart?

we know you will never really retire.
there is fire
on the path to freedom.
there is smoke, there is sacrifice.
there are stories of justice. of women.
of Tubman. of Truth. of Angela and Assata.
Coretta and Merlie. Betty and Queen Mother Moore.

some of us know we are ancient
that our marrow is laced with legacy
that we are here to bring life to daughters.

sometimes it just takes one woman.
a mother
a grandmother
a spit-fire griot. a sista.
the only woman to lead the NAACP's largest Chapter.
she. daughter of the movement. of Rosa. of Erma.
she was a birth that gave birth to possibility
for other young activists.
a true D woman. frontline Fatima. Nigerian blood.
councilwoman. leader. truth teller.
Jo Ann Watson. social worker.
president of the anti-klan network.
sister. inspiration. dedicated to the protection of girls &

the voices of women. wrapped in west african beauty.
regal and resilient.
wake up Detroit
wake up South Africa
wake up Cuba
wake up small business owners
wake up white house
wake up reparations
wake up teachers/wake up women/wake up schools

sleeping is not an option with
The Honorary Jo Ann Watson
in the room.

Damn**Right**

(After Razor) Dedicated to Imamu Amiri Baraka.
Read at his Memorial Service at Newark Symphony Hall
January 9, 2014. For Ras, Mama Amina, and the entire Baraka
family

the death of my father at 69
reminds me
that every new year
is a kiss from god

or maybe it is simply a reminder
that catching bullets in our teeth
are not just for comic book super heroes
that literary giants also battle
against the monstrous heads of
connie and bil
and survive, unscathed.

attention critics from nowhere.
u might be forced to wear your spine to work. today.

Amiri Baraka is busy with a higher calling.

somebody gotta ask
who gonna be the messengers?

where is Sun Ra?
where are the holy ghosts
our prophets?

wise why's y
do they call us hip hop
or say we slam

when we r your students. Baraka.
the invisible ones
the spooks that knocked down doors
we don't juggle or hop scotch or jump through fire

we write.

we know your bright suns have plans for this mourning
we know your daughters are re-imagining the night
others began writing our suicide letters for us

a long time ago.

ignoring the young cultural revolutionaries
u taught us how
to breathe inside the polluted
cesspool of segregated libraries.
in the name of Baraka

we dance. we teach.
we tear down. we build up.
we believe in the face of the faithless.

we move for those who be stiff
we fly for those who be still
we have no choice.

he created this fire
who gonna keep it lit?

Scholar with sword. Master teacher
with miracles as metaphor.

who's gonna call the ignorant *ignorant*
to their faces on national television?

who gonna make love inside a 8 bar blues?

here comes the heart
here come our cities
here come the people

u don't have to explain your chakras

just breathe
here comes Baraka
damn right
here comes injustice
damn right
here comes protest

here comes the hat tilt
here comes the b boy stance
here comes freedom
here comes peace

who's gonna spike the tea?
who's gonna plant a poem and grow a life?
who's gonna bring the scholars
out their ivory tower prisons?

who's gonna call a spade a King and
out joke the joker?

who's gonna build the low ku bombs?

with the world and our bookshelves
dying a little more
every day

who gonna teach the children?
who gonna rebel?

who gonna go into our prisons?

where

r our redemption songs

now

?

we conjuring the whole truth of language
from the scraps of a twisted alphabet
the chitterling backwash taste of bitter standardized
testing and watered down curriculums

we are the economy of pyramids
the who we be's
and the what we did's.

we what they thought
was hid.

damn right
these words don't fit
damn right
the records skip

when your life is a calling
when the ancestors have prepared you
for the politricks

how do u pick the red pill or the whitest fence
when our cities are born with the bluest eyes
the darkest tales and the most beautiful African
people who don't know they is Africans.

who's cutting the grass of
the killing fields?

the dream dealers, the beat creators
the painters, the poets, the movement
people
the truth tellers, the lovers, the liars

oh, bless u, the liars

who's blues they gonna steal

Now.

?

Which names they gonna mispronounce
leave out, set back, pretend not to know?

He created this fire.
who gon' keep it lit

Huh?

who's gonna print the books

who's gonna program the silences

who's gonna own the bookstores

who's gonna burn the house down

who gonna tell em
the revolution is your mirror

?

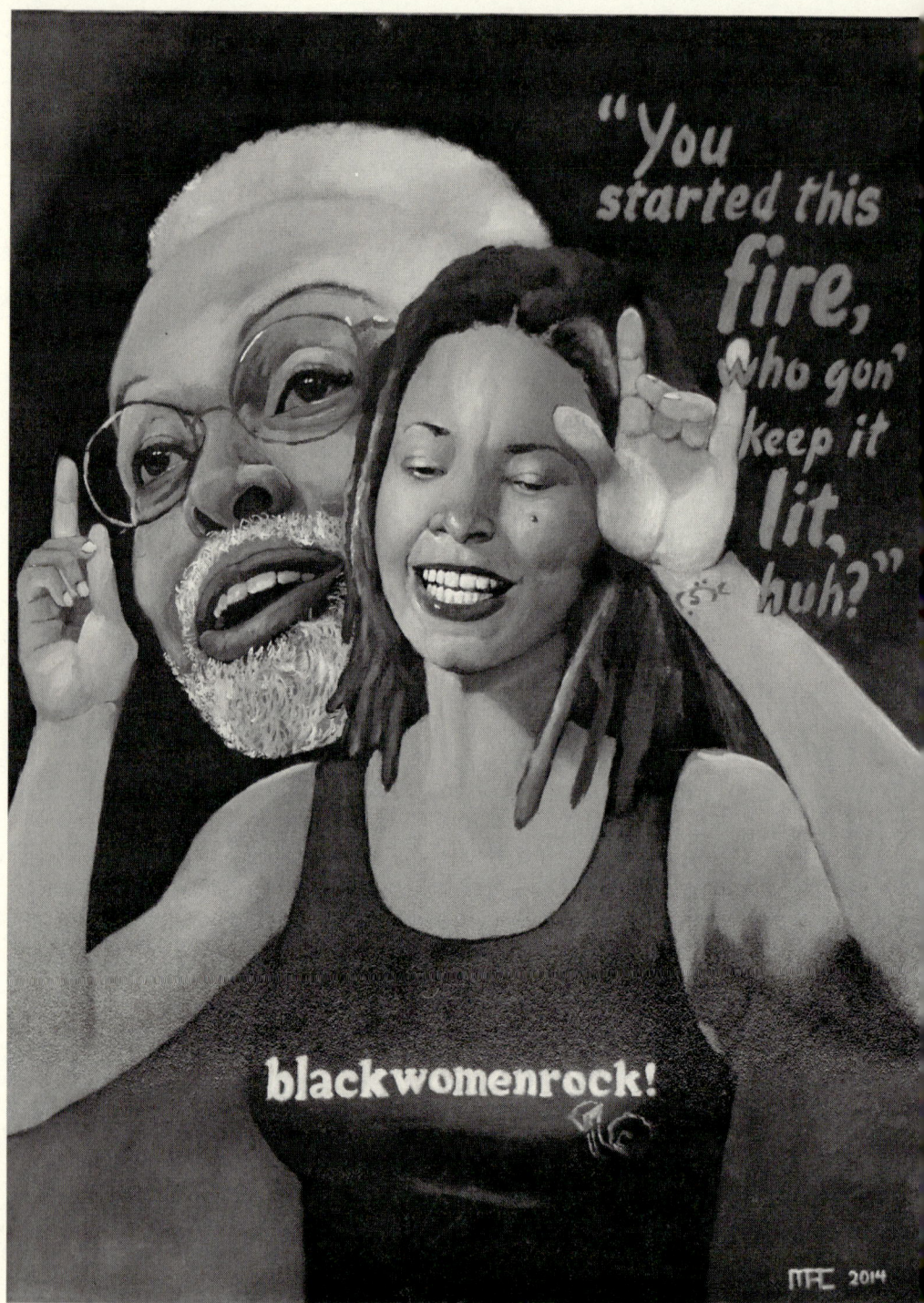

"Legends" (Amiri Baraka and jessica Care moore © 2014 Michael Angelo Chester
Oil on canvas.

He created this fire.

who's gonna keep it lit

huh?

Baraka black Baraka jazz
Baraka blues Baraka danced
'til there were no shoes to drag

where u from?

detroit-newark-harlem-tuskegee-berlin-palestine

who gonna fill the ark with art?
who gonna be the new?

who gonna recognize the old?
who gonna identify your soul?

spirit don't lie
but the papers   do.

who gonna control
who remember you.
me. me. us us we we.

damn right

your stories are that of a lion
on the frontline of an american schizophrenic jungle
prophet footing and warrior ink blood.

they cannot kill us all

with their black face and tragic twisted
imitations of life
we understand

Amiri Baraka has
out lived your double cross.

his books held political prisoner by
un-established unsophisticated establishments
we hold his words as

armor

as a symbol of our fearlessness

we ask his children, his wife Amina
for permission to claim him

we smile his boyish grin
waiting for the low-ku
bomb to
drop.

he teaches us there is jazz playing
every time the sun rises
a jackal of words
a blues man with his hat always in place
you

father of movement and possibility
Baraka black and artistic
handing out pamphlets
full of rebellion and resistance

we know your lifework
is simply an answer to a question

why God?
why Ancestors?
why Malcolm?

why Langston?

why Jayne?

why Lucille?
why Haki?
why Askia?
why Gil?
why Sonia?
why Last Poets?

(why asha why tony why saul why thomas why mike why kevin
why ekere why ursula why lamar why willie why carl why major
why leeza)

why ancestors

why brilliant
why organizer
why fathers
why uncles
why scholars
why essayist
why teacher
why legacy
why blk genius

why Baraka?

why God?

why in the hell did you have to make

me

a poet?

and God replied,

Leroi, somebody had to show them how to do it.

a **different kind** of **power**

i see my son's locs long as expressways swirling into a constant set of
questions. King is 7 years old and he wants to know if this is a dream
state. For my son King and my sons and daughters in Chicago, Il.

I dream of a place where I can
simply raise my native son to be human.
To love music. To make art.
To fall in love and to make things
he loves   with his hands.

I Am Not Urban Fiction.
My blood is blue and tastes sweet as
A Huntsville watermelon.
I have seen black seeds spit out and left to die in my arms.
I have buried blood, bitter, before it was truly ripe.
I have become a hardened, green Rind.
Too numb to death. Too cold to swallow.
I don't want to raise another necessary warrior.
A black man on constant defense.
Is that weak? Feminine? Delusional?
Maybe in Detroit. St Louis. Chicago.
This is just a dream. A mother's heart. A naivety.
A nerve forgotten.

I want to tell our boys i see the Ogun Iron walk in you.
The Kwame Toure fire in you
I want to tell our daughters. that i know the source
of your internal bruises. i know that a brown girl's pain passes
down quietly through our families like hand me down heels
that don't fit and enter your girlhood

at knife/point

We are killed with no large community outcry.

You are more than a pole dancer or the mirror.
These haunted magazine covers
make u believe. Their make/believe.

Nothing about you is ugly. Holy water princess
Oya eyes. Yemaja swimming in your womb.
Castles for legs running water past everything
& every corner
they said u weren't gonna be
or ever turn.
Beautiful. but you are. Coal heart shining
The bling is buried deep
in the marrow of your bones
beneath the surface of your skin.
Chin up warrior. Young goddesses in pigtails.

They turned double dutch into iambic pentameter
so u cldn't even find the poem you wrote.
They thought we wldn't find you

Concrete flowers with stemmed spines

But i see you. Fumbling with mis-education &
How many times have you been called what U.R. not?

We need you to collect our breath & milk
inside mason jars.

There are women who've been writing about you.
Waiting for you. Daughters of Zora and Bambara
Sanchez and Brooks.

There are no iron chefs that can burn
stories the way sistas can cook with pens
with maps, with a turn of a head, the colossal

push of our hips to birth a nation.

Young Malcolms and Turners and you turn
on us. On yourselves. In the name of land
you don't own. Your fight is not for our people
but with your own people.

We sacrifice our cervix to fix the future.
We need you to make it there.

You are the masters of this universe
the imagination of Octavia
the truth of Sojourner
Collector of butterflies and cocoons
 just waiting to happen.

I was 17 when I realized I cld save the lives
of all my male friends
by closing my legs and making them love me
enough so they would listen
when I said "No, you cannot go shoot up that house
with your boys tonight. I need you
to stop
chasing death."

We walk in a place that detached our legs from
Trees that bore strange fruit &
gave birth to blues.

Are we to push them back up into our wombs?
To save them from a life of inhumanity?
Where is the Sonia Sanchez haikued
vision of peace?

I'm tired of black boys being treated like
a pack of pit bulls.

I don't want to be afraid of my own sons.

Is that too much to ask?
I'm simply attempting to give my
Beautiful spirited son

A different kind of power.

I take full responsibility for my mythology & dreams & the confusion & pain & art that comes from all of it.

cashing in

Cashing in 90,000 sky miles won't make him fall in love.
You better fall in love with yourself. Again. Girl. A poet will chase
love to the bottom of the gutter/cross thousands of miles of ocean just
for the thought that something/someone real was waiting upon
landing.

There was a landing. There is peace in rejection. I am not for
everyone. I am not everyone's kind of woman but I am certain I am
some kind of woman. I cannot understand men who don't hold a
woman's hand. It's rejecting God to not touch palms. My journey to
Hong Kong was a return to myself.

When I returned from my first trip to Asia, I would tattoo "Wisdom
and Growth" on my left wrist in Arabic. I needed a reminder to always
be open to being whimsical and dreamy about love/while never
forgetting that loving another is first about truly loving yourself.

Writing on the plane in route to Hong Kong Delta Flight 187 (great)

poet with sky miles

"The wound is the place where the light enters you"

—*Rumi*

I won't convince the revolutionary to leave the revolution.
We Babylon destroyers. The closest approximation to God is love.
Still, we often forget. Fire Tongues. Desert Sand. Sleeping in the
memory of our brown fingers.

Our ancestors saved us for a reason.

It is not to hide inside our skin or be something we
were not destined to be.
We are after-all born to see what they cannot.

How can I speak to you in plain English? A non-language.
This is not a love poem. I assure you. It is a promise.
A doctrine of Haiku. A remembrance. I
heard you. *You know me.* So, I heard you.

Moving time is the work of the unseen. I am never afraid of
my kindred spirits. My tribe of freedom walkers. The truth makes me cry.
I too have seen death. I've cried from knowing too much and wanted
to see the blood of revolution at it's feet. It is difficult to be born again.
When you feel someone misplaced your eyes. At nine years old, I
recognized my fascination with life. In a constant state of déjà vu, I
wanted to save animals. My infatuation with the sun. A sun I
attempted to face. A sun I tried to pray toward. So many prayers
rugs…catholic school…and personal alters for Oya…finding
Buddha…Me,
a daughter of God without indoctrination.

I was born a mother. I know I'm a nation builder. I know I've saved
the lives of our brothers my whole life. Before I left Detroit (this time),
after I asked him to take care of Nana, my son asked me,
"Who's gonna take care of you mommy?"
My brilliant son. This is the answer of the century.
King replied, "Mommy I will take care of you."

I understand my role of inspiration. As girl. As daughter of words.
As lover. As your lover. Though we have not touched or kissed.

We already a birth. A beginning. A laugh. A freedom. A joy.
A forgotten childhood. The opening scenes of my favorite films
you sent me in Harlem. A place we will visit in South Carolina one day.
You promise. A place we have already been. You will be a carpenter.
I will be a teacher. Maybe I will paint. While you cook and play guitar,
I will take orders at our restaurant. King will learn all my secrets and
bury our recipes in a jar
deep inside some fertile red clay.

I will swallow your laugh to feed past pain and I will hold you
until I've gone numb and my arms melt into my wrist. We will win by
dancing with stars and your artist heart will somehow see the urgency
of our own personal army.

Our future children's children. We will adopt soldiers as angels.

Light as speech. Keepers of dragons.
Butterflies collapsing from exhaustion.

Perhaps there is an answer to the blues.

We cry. Carve out lives out of fear.

Whatever God Wills.

Is not just a phrase, but the question of how we
Will choose to live our lives.

I only ask that you show up honestly.

When we meet again.

On this foreign island.

This place we spend my days as your nights, blurring into
Good mornings and never minds. There is no space. No time.
No language. No time. No poems.

What if our feet could sing and our hearts could cook
and our intentions were actions and
our beauty was self-evident?

What if poetry was dialogue?

Laughter, required for breathing.

What if we moved as we spoke.

This is not a letter. Or a speech. Promises are for my young sons.
I too have seen God. My hair silver/blue on Mondays.
I am Seven. I am pigtails and politics.
I am this heart beating. In your hands.

I am the girl next door. In search of a boy
Who can talk to me about Clarke
Teach me pieces of fluent Arabic
Debate Malcolm and Dubois
Show me how to doug-e
And walk and talk fast as me.

Someone who can sharpen the edge of my sword and
Understand my weapons are kept in my hair. Tender. So tender.
Despite the sharpness of my tongue.

Marsh/mallow. You can see it. My vertigo legs relaxing at 33 flights up.
Protected by the pull of a simple green string. I follow.
Travel the gentleness you placed on my wrist.

A set of trees lying on my blue veins. Blue as this ocean.
This ocean is crossing me. I travel in circles.
Sankofa lipped. Poetry armed. Anticipating the greatest
Revolution ever won. When the Queen finds the King.
Removed French Africans. Reincarnated as conductors
Of an underground railroad. Stop.

Motor City twilight children crooning with Ruffin and
Sleeping with Smokey. Organizing take-overs and
Becoming frontline committed to
Returning to our proper position as chosen people.

Carriers of light. These bodies. Protected by bone and muscle.
Translated in Sanskrit. Traces of Arabic. You sometimes find.
It never really leaves. I was never a temporary spirit.
I'm returning as Yasmine. Re/locating myself.
In the middle of April

What else are we to do with

Spring?

I wish I could write this poem in Chinese

I have run out of haiku
The plight of my story cannot
Be confined inside structure.

Run jessica run.
Always in the wrong direction
Trying to save someone from themselves
Never preserving my heart.

Falling is a weapon against me
I feel beautiful in my 40th year
I've grown accustomed to giving myself
Compliments, and not waiting for men
To find one.

It's not vanity, but an act of survival.

Yellow lilacs take over this space
33 floors above the ground.
The higher up, the more human
I suppose.
I kiss his nose. Examine his feet.
I'm trying to get him to recognize me
In my new skin.
It is difficult.
He is a guarded fire.
I am water, waiting for the flame.
Holding him is holding God.
My vertigo tears drop over the balcony.
The sun is shining in Hong Kong
I need to be near a body of water.
The China Sea.
The Amazon River.

It is healing to be close to something

That frightens you.

He says he is not scared.

I am not afraid of loving this man
I am only afraid of him not loving me
In return.

Just once. I'd like to get it right.
We so close. We family.
He is trying to figure out who I am.
Daughter. Cousin. Sister.

I do the math. Addition.

Wife?

Past Life Lover?

We hold hands and when he
Let's go

I exhale and practice walking

I have New York legs and navigation skills.

Breathing is a craft I'm still perfecting.
Patience becomes him.

I am lotus.
Taupe petals across his floor.
Poems fall like stars
From his eyes and land inside
My hands.

I've never felt so safe
This high up.

2:04 p. m hk time april 14th.

the cat in the window
for Zaid

Is yellow. The people
Hang their clothes from
The 45th floor.

A trusted balcony. A bamboo
Tightrope. There is balance
Among the clouds.

The cat watches the man in
White boxers. Nothing to do.

Pastel blue and green curtains
Accent the Queen's sometimes English
In Chinese.
The letters are a song. A hymn.
Polite and sweet. I try on a hat
On the MTR. You are very beautiful.
The sales girl greets me.

I see Mongolian noses and slanted
Brown eyes that look like my own.

I am a red/light brown/yellow girl

Quite at home around a language made of
Artistic lines and variations of sound.

I plan to see Buddha.
Place lilacs in my hair
For the night.

I am a star watcher. He calls me a star.

I am simply a cat.
Counting lives. Saving lives.
Writing poems above people
Was never my intention.

I am a Langston cat. An Amiri Cat. A Sonia Cat.
A Haki Cat. An Abiodun Cat. A Cortez Cat.

And being black always

Brought me luck and sometimes a lottery number
Inside this fortune cookie existence.

I've attempted to live
And sometimes we've died
In the name of poems.

11:52 a.m. Hong Kong. April 13th.

haikus

resistance haiku
face covered legend
     cherokee techno language
     ancient wax, i am

madness is an art form
music code breaker
     resist mediocrity
     genius is now born

untitled
     how many hearts you take
     what did you sacrifice, huh?
     my pain made that   beat.

Balance
     walk slow. on purpose
     earth still spins. on it's axis
     why rush to red lights?

he said
> sex is not for sport
> sometimes there is love. he said.
> my heart forms a sound

the future of baseball
> if my plane don't land
> make sure king keeps his first glove
> teach him. to catch. love.

on pawning diamonds
> i've been married. twice.
> worn red. thrown rice. jumped brooms. cried.
> now i just want. peace.

Moore/Joy
for Justin Rice Moore
> You hold my hand. with
> ease. we. a familiar river. loud &
> quiet at once. we dance at red lights.
> bee gees on repeat. we laugh.
> you paint. i poet.
> we both fighting the good fight.
> we strike. a necessary fire.
> you/match   me
>
> on the inside.

deepbreath

it's taken me 40 yrs
to learn how to breathe.   properly.
maybe now i will find a poem   worth recording

the pace you learn in time.
my new york walk on pause.
as your palms
hold my waist and teach
me to push calm inside my legs
find peace by protecting what naturally
helps us live.

i read my poems 700 mph
a predator of words
metaphors soaked in blood & tears
& the lie of a girl who says sex is
recreational when
our heart chakras are the most tender
the most vulnerable place for a man to enter
without protection

some pretend to know how to breathe
when we are really existing on held back pain
too scared to push out the truth
that got us into womanhood
we replace our femininity with male bravado
forgetting out Goddess & forsaking our future
warrior daughters

this cherokee mississippi man with southern blues
on saturn genius
detroit great lakes waters running through
his michigan

left hand.
i kiss his right cheek and think of catching
a fish to cook him

in a safe place.

i wonder if he can see his children when he looks
through me...

we wish we'd met sooner

but here we are in this ancient space.
on a hill discovering breath, honesty and balance.
the weight of every scar balanced above my head.
my heart breaks 'round & steel in my left .

i am not moved or shaken easily.
even the hopeless romantic has moments of retreat.
i repeat my breathing
and attempt to have casual conversations with a man
who reminds me of me.

i roll my native eyes back to a time of simpler living.
a red cardinal lands on my porch after a morning rain.

a ladybug interrupts our exchange at the bottom of the

hill.

our hands, a mountain for this 17 black dotted insect.
legs kissing my fingers.

beauty is such a small, intimate thing.

white clouds of mercy take over the turquoise sky.
a softball yellow as the sun finds form inside my glove

& connects to a tickled catcher. finally she finds her
rhythm. pulls up her leg. loose wrist.

core straight. aimed. pulls back the mit.
deep breath.

the neon sun flies straight for his hands.
he doesn't miss.

he is rooted, grounded in this field.
she dreams.
she will be the lighting strike.
he didn't let get away

this time.

traveling **moon**

For all my students in St. Louis I met while teaching through Prison Performing Arts and the women inmates in Vandalia, MO who continue to inspire me.

So I said to myself
Girl that man has a lot on his plate
Don't be bothering him with

Dreams & poems too
Damn early for all that

I've been alive in this life
For forty years

Life is so fragile
So short
So sweet

My hotel offers a pretty
Good $5 breakfast

This is not country oven
No sexy old women
No bottomless coffee
No smell of Detroit funk

Today I will teach these
Young prisoners peace.

As I attempt to find some
Can't get Deotray's face outta my
Head.

I never want to become numb to death
I never want to become numb to love

No matter what this day, this week
Attempts to do to your spirit

Know there is a poet
Protecting you with words
An invisible armor

I don't have on my poker face
arms, mouth, heart or hands
With you.
I never do.
I wear my mornings on my sleeve
I know the night is full of games
& sometimes

there is the traveling moon.
\
My breakfast plate is clean
& white.

& missing

Our post hill
conversations

That carry me past the
Mediocrity of mornings
& boredom that comes
With thinking fast
in a slowed
Down place.

The race is always with

Ourselves. Dear brother. Friend.
Twin spirit. Revolutionary. Partner.

Today I will tell them
As they resist & struggle
With the idea of living in peace.

Love will never be
a thing

of the past.

When the day begins and ends with
fireworks

I have been a hurricane.
Katrina.
A tornado dancing through southern
shot gun houses. You. Native Nile
Quiet Lion smiling
Amazon river laugh
Curious how you cld find a way to bend
down so close to my
eye level.
Tall/Midwest/Charmer

I should be running in the other direction
I'm training for my first half marathon.
I can't remember the last time
I was literally lifted off my feet
experienced a long goodbye
or listened to the sound of a man
fall sleeping after a five hour phone
call at 4 a.m.

My body is officially leaving
but the rest of me is waiting

to see u again.

Have mercy. Have flowers.
I must leave this city where there are no strangers
& the summer is much too short.

I am breaking earth
I am wearing high heels at noon.

I am late for my appointments

Mondays feel like Saturdays

The Queendom was patiently waiting
40 years for you to finally
cross the half court line

so i cld simply

      shoot   your   lights
                       out!

      FireWorks.

no encore

no **encore**

*for Jose James, after his looped performance of Strange Fruit
on Billie's Birthday
Brussels April 7, 2012.*

I told the man from Africa. You don't have to be from Africa
To be an African. I'm a pre-slave ship African. My people.
Our people. Native. Our people on that ship. Narratives are
Complex. Layered.

Brown lover. Red lover.

On my honor I will try. It's my duty to be done and I say I.

He doesn't believe the girl scout in me. Even with sage breath
And the sun directly in his eyes.

I have known you. Conjurer of all things living.
My arms, think black licorice. Bending. Growing. New fruit.
Every time the moon appears. Bluescology.

Heart directly to hands
These tears you shed as sacrifice. Blood still raining from leaves
This is not make believe. This ain't a jazz standard. This is Europe.
This is so very American.
Politics.

You/walk in coolly. On Billie's birthday.
We wear struggle like new shoes. We the joy only found
In the gutter of pain. Your salted high cheeks. Kissed by God.
Is it possible to just be an artist anymore?

Brown?
Borrowed. Stolen. Threatened. Loved. Adored. Worshipped.

Feared. Never lie on the stage
And you will be forgiven.

Never lie on the page. A tree gave her life 4 you.
The least you cld do is get on your knees & write an honest
Poem/song

Prayer.

Tattoo the words round your neck. For protection.

Kiss your work in the mouth
While the world's watching/waiting
Écoutez mi amour
They can't kill what they will
Never understand
Coded laughter. Champagne tongues.
Ice on burning skin.
This is redemption. This is the epitome of sin
When an eternity is hidden inside 24 hour days

When revolution is a chapter of a book
Never sent to print.
My digitized palms simply want to find a shorter
Forked line to truth. Perhaps the people behind the times
Are before their time in the future. My pace matches your
Heart. I'm beating. I'm writing. I'm fighting.

We are all dying to live.

I forgive.

Start with yourself first. You can't keep pushing silence
Outta your womb.
Birth is noisy. Messy. A spirit awakening.
A crossing over.

The way kissing you makes
My body numb for a few seconds before the blood
Rushes back in.

& the poem begins
& the dancers stretch
& the mics get checked
& the wine is poured
& the trumpet coughs
& lynching is theater
& our future children are forgotten

Inside the rotting of an old testament apple
There is our brilliant core.

In the cotton fields of someone else's soft place to dream
We scream. We sing.

& they stand.

On corners.

We die

On corners

Encore.

No more encores
No more encores

No more clapping
No more rebellion concerts
No more bows in solidarity
No more poetic realism

I will leave this stage. Forever.
Cutting at my soles as I walk
I promise to never speak to you
in riddles & hold you
This is not an underground
Rail/road\
Stop
No encores
No shows
No more black face
No more corporate white hoods
Love exits. Stage right.

Tenderly

Till we leave

these blues

for good.

when **I write** there is **light**

for asha bandele

when i write there is light.
there is a rush and sometimes
there is nothing at all.

there are hours of calm and then
nights are sleepless. it is cold and i can
see beyond the limits of the naked eye.

stars are closer than they seem.

sometimes i smoke for the oral fix.
tea is necessary.
a healing. a part of the writing. a part of the
telling. i don't expect to be well
liked. awarded. i am loved by enough humans
to satisfy an alien ego.

i am so many women. i have prayed
with palms up.
head to the floor.
in yoga stance. in my hands. crying.
i have cursed. sinned in the language
of the sinners. i don't believe the beliefs are
believable. i don't believe love
is ever trouble. even when the timing is off.

i am often on time for my own scenes.
but getting the other players to know
their lines to make my film fantastic, well
that becomes the achilles.

i'm addicted to running a specific hill.

i turn down so many men. i am lonely on purpose.
alone by choice. i really am never going to be alone.
everyone is always listening. repeating. dreaming
it was them doing your life. this life is a fraction
of what my expectation is
for myself.

i'm always falling in love. in full color.
i fall in love in seconds. it is
a rush. if i am not writing about you
i'm bored. i can smell insecurity.

i can hear it with the questions i
refuse to answer.

if i love you i will
sleep in your shirt.

i am becoming afraid of my elders leaving
me without me writing my best work.
poems are protection. my property. the
things i pull off and put into a box.
i will claim them when i'm allowed out of this
place. put my pony tail back in place. put my gold
egyptian switch blade back
in my pocket. the swiss army my current love
bought me. i want all my sharp
edge. softened. for the blow. the need. the high.

the writing. it hurts when i'm
typing. today i am afraid. i am thinking of
jayne. i am thinking of sonia. i am
wondering about my body. who will touch this work.
when i'm gone.

i'm afraid to write. i'm so full of fear.

but i write anyway. because i have no
other way to participate in this realm of existence.
how do i exist? how have i fed my sons
on poems. what does that taste like. that's not a question so
there is no question mark. we are full. electric words.
on fire. i drink fire/water. they ate all my words.
now they both paint.
i visualized motherhood.
i have survived deep pains.
extreme losses.
i'm just beginning.
what could i possibly write that is
of any worth?

i'm too young to be taken too seriously.
i'm too old to be ignored. what is
the work, when it's inside the writing. i am
blue collar. working class.

nobody ever gave me a dime and
said, "simply write"

but it doesn't stop me from writing. from making breath
and bread outta vowels.

i've never been endowed a smile. and no special movement
vowed to give support for my nouns or my bowels.
shit. keep the writing easy.
everyone is uneasy. but they invited me to
this facade.

it is so much easier to be a ghost. or a liar.
liars make large amounts of
money. i cannot lie and write at the same time.
it's difficult for me to relate
to young women. even though i'm a young woman.

i have lived so many lives. i don't write that to
sound like it's some kind of profundity. it is just
what it is. i am a wife. i am a lover. i am a mother.
so many moments. names.
schools. countries. hopeless romantic stories.

how is it possible to feel as if my heart has been
pulled from my body & still want this senseless
painful organ to make music. it is a soundtrack. a necessary
note. a deranged blood pump. an apple. my core.
it's where all my children were
born.

"When is the last time you really turned her on?"

Nothing happens between our legs

this is the mythology of men.
this is their twisted erotica.
everything erotic about a woman happens
inside her chest & above her neck.
only real men know this.
cowboys & indians.
i am a predator.
i know when i want something. any man.
and when i don't
i feel nothing. if i can't imagine a kiss
then there is nothing
to imagine.

the poems come fast and so do they.

the great ones get past a few stanzas
and then it's over.
they only show up for the haiku.
it's easier that way.

great title. three lines. nature.
who can fuck that up?

i am so delicate when haiku like.

calculated.
polite.
controlled.
structured.

when is the writing the disguise?
the costume to win the grant. i never
win those contests. i will not write in their words
to get my words recognized as
valuable.

this is my gift. this is my work. this is what i will do
until i die. all my grants have been given by God.

i have a magical life.

it is not easy. magic. it's not something you whip
up in a pot. it is applied
genius. it is the humility of the sun setting.
it is the arrogance of the sky
dropping down clouds to remind us of the
fog.
forgive us.
forgive me.

it has nothing to do with your writing.
it was your video. it has nothing to
do with your video. it was the way you quietly said
fuck you underneath it all and
maybe they heard it.
it was written as a whisper.

i hate the word *hate* but i hate *transparency* more.

nothing i write or do with my hands

will ever be

trans/parent.

i ride horses in my head and on my city street.
i am surrounded by angels.
this is not the end of the world.
how many suns will my sons see in their lifetime?
how dare you write us out of
our memory.
i remember the future. and she
shines. and so does he.
the world is renewed.

i'm drinking chocolate. i see the man who thinks
women
my age become invisible
when young men can no longer see us.
he has no idea how much i long for the
day when all those eyes are finally off my skin.

he says i'm beautiful all the time and it
has no meaning.
so what?
beautiful & useless.

i want to be plugged into your skin.
be turned on by subtle conversation. gentle
kisses. made beautiful.
surface royalty is just that.
i never enjoyed being called

Queen.
some things don't need to be said.

i need movement. verbs.
let's make something beautiful.
that's a compliment.
that's complex.
that's everything.

i need a space filled.
i need a glass raised.
i'm gonna need your planet pulled
a lot closer to mine.

i'm dating outside my planet.
i'm writing inside. i'm waiting. outside.
always waiting
for the poem.

i live between the them.
the line breaks are my deepest breaths.

it's true honest johns.

men lie and they are still so beautiful.
women love and they are the core of an apple.
skin peeled. curious. open.
first fruits.
diamond tongue.

i never imagined a kiss
in a face like yours.
i'm a lover of wolves.
moon rum. drinking the night.
conjuring the sun.

i cannot see or sit or talk with people
talking about talking.
doing nothing.
mouth full of coffee and riddles and
no sweat no grind.

every corner is a poem in this city.

always so pin drop dark
when everyone else is sleeping.

that's when i write.

God.

please

when I wake up

let there be

light.

sunlight through bullet holes

I don't believe that women have gone mad,
I believe the world has gone mad.
As for men,
they've reinvented the asylum.

—*Jessi James*

sunlight through bullet holes

This is a bus with wings
Flying me high above the earth
I need red clay forgiveness
I need a Nina Simone gun
With no bullets
Just fire
Just freedom

I bite down hard on my bottom lip
To remind myself of the pain
To feel something soft on my
Body filled with concrete, metal
And somebody else's needles.

I am a shadow of myself.
I am the after hour party
The next stop is my stop
Any stop. Just don't stop
Keep driving bus driver
Till we touch the first
Cloud in the entrance to
Heaven.

There has to be a safe place
For women who had a yesterday
And a series of uncertain
Tomorrows.
This window is the entire
World. Maybe the earth is
Flat and square after all.

Maybe I would stop running
In circles if I just went to
The edge of this mutha fucka
And jumped.

This is better than jumping.
This is a church revival. Ooh. Baby.
They could never save me in those

Pretty places. Too much stained
Glass. I need to be able to see
Inside.

I wanna hear my God in a simple place.
The loud speaker at a drive through menu.
There u are. I can hear you talking to me.
I love French fries. Always have. I can
Fix a lot things about myself. That one
I ain't changing.
Changing. What the hell is that anyway ?
We all the same from the moment we are born.
Aren't we?
I'm moving, but I'm still me. I don't have a
Costume. Not for this life. I will ask God
For a new one next time around, maybe.
Change is good. Things we can't control we
Name good. Getting high is good, when u can
Control it. Check that out.

I just want to eat and sleep for a few months. Wake up
As a movie star in a different film.
Maybe more meat to cover these bones.
This is not my movie. I had to convince myself.
So here I am, a jar full of empty promises
And letters never sent.
I couldn't hold him. I didn't know how to hold him.
Who was gonna hold me? Huh?

Why we only born with these two hands anyway.
Explain that shit to me. Women need more than two.
What is someone cuts these off. It happens.

Or arms. They can just fall off from exhaustion.
What's up modern medicine?
Help me grow some new arms!
Why can't we just grow new ones?
Humans ain't so special.
Can't just heal our wounds by a touch or a kiss.
That's never enough.
We gotta take pills to fix our brains.
We so smart, we don't know how to
Think

Without some help.
That's all I need. A little help.

A cross to bear. A bridge to cross.
I am not broken. Just tired.
Damaged slightly.
Nothing good lasts forever.
And sometimes nothing bad does either.
This is my stop. Can we land now
Bus driver?
That old bridge exists in the reflection
Of the new. Simply beautiful. I need

To sleep somewhere like that.
I need to wake up in the care of the sun.
I need to feel safe with my eyes closed.
I need to land. Like an alley cat.
I paid my fare a million times.
I am not a secret!!
I am screaming
Inside this shell.
Time can't find me here. No more
Watches. Everybody watches.

Watch me get off.
Watch me get off.
Watch me land.
I got wings
This bus got wings.
Just put this baby in drive.
And let's fly
Let's exist together
For the very first

time.

L'**Union** Fait **La Force**
a poem for Haiti

Being black and free
Is a fragile state.
We. With indigo blood.
Cotton tongues.
Cacao skin.
We. Simmering beneath the fire
Of a 1791 brewed coffee
We. Like the cruelty of bitter sweet sugarcane fields.
That plantation. Our children's
Voices and teeth.

We. Still being pulled from beneath our homes.
We. Displaced. Unsure if our families are dead.
We want to see their bodies. We want proof.
We want them back.
We know pride can get you killed.
We. Children of somebody's gifted God.
We the Ancient African.
We. Who saved you from slavery.
We. Who understood our value
Before being a global citizen
Was en vogue.

We with nothing to do but survive.
Rebuild our communities.
Put food on our families tables.

We are millions, homeless at home.
Digging ourselves, away from the
Dead, the dehydrated, the unborn, the delivered.

We are the holy ghost believers.
We are the holders of ancient ritual and truth.

What is the formula for this level of mourning?
How do we articulate the numbing, the confusion,
The trauma of war, of natural disaster.

There is no easy way to speak about the violence of rape.
A universal crime against women and girls, increases
Daily in camps as we drink and party and
Complain about the recession and our mortgages.

This is a test of our humanity on the world stage.
Who shall we blame, as we are opened up again
Meteor sized holes in the hearts of our capital city
We forget that death is a problem
For the living.

We. Ocean People.
We simply need clean water for our babies.
Haiti/gave us Julie. She is a nurse. At 21. She didn't
Need to take a board test to be certified in the
United States, because in Haiti the
Free nursing program was unparallel.
She knew Haiti as a beautiful place.
With good food and perfectly warm nights.
She is the daughter of La Vallee De Jacmel
Let me tell you.
They don't show the beauty on the news.
She dreams of the countryside where we fed ourselves.
From our own farms. When Haitians bought rice from
Haitians. Before the factories and US interest and imports.
She remembers a people that used to fish and waited
For no one to do anything for them.

Colonization is not new news.
Haiti is no longer headline news.

Guetty. A brown starry-eyed Haitian filmmaker has
Returned home to a night that is still and quiet
Her heart is sleeping in her memory. This blinding light
A half moon mirror, covers and reflects
A broken, but resilient city.

Disorganization from non-governmental organizations
Bring confusion and indifference.
There is little or no effective relief effort in place,
After a year.

She is asking us. American Africans to stand up
For Haiti. She is asking us to remember her forefathers
Who snatched their independence from the French
And brought back 800 American Slaves to Haiti
To live free.

She is asking us to make a promise to
The people who promised to fight for the freedom

Of the African Diaspora/ to help rebuild.

She is asking us to simply become the people
We say we are on
Sunday mornings at our churches.
Saturday at our synagogues.
After Juma on Fridays.

What do the God fearing fear, if there is
No place for the children of Abraham
And Moses?

Which new religion has no place for the poor?

We. Too rich. Too self consumed.
To see ourselves. Our own children dying

From dehydration and hopelessness in our
Own arms.

The nurse's son is now a man. Traveling
From Brooklyn to Haiti
8 days after the earthquake.
Organizing the shipment of
Medical supplies and unassembled tents
Sitting in an airport for days. Untouched.

Where are you Toussaint L'Ouverture of 1804?
My removed symbol of Haiti has always been
One of courage.

In March, there was, is still, little relief on the ground.
As he continued his job of removing debris for the
Reconstruction of schools.
Dismembered brick with no direction, no place.
Just piled
In the streets blocking traffic where volunteers attempted to
Get to the Epicenter.

We eat well with taped American mouths
While the Haitian lower middle class
Suffers from the red sticky unorganized ugly of politics.
We cannot run
From our own history repackaged and sold to us
By outsiders. Boken down into
21st century caste systems.
The new gentrified slavery is alive in
Brooklyn, Detroit, Chicago.

You haven't seen it?

The natural disaster will not be in the cracked earth of
This beautiful, resourceful country.

It will be in the turned back bend of an inevitable
After-shock of abandonment by the
Wealthy Corrupt
World Governments.

Cholera is not going to infect or kill more
Than half a million people in Haiti.

But not having health care will.

We. Are the Ancestors of a
Just Do Culture.
We the offspring of optimism
We. The rebellious line of plantation burners.
We. Practitioners of Voudoun.
We. the deities of forgiveness
We. Sequined stories beaded inside the
Flags of artist, Jean Joseph Jean-Baptiste
We the rebellious line of the forsaken.
We the language of Kreyol
We ten thousands seven hundred and fourteen
Miles of black nationhood.
We destiny driven. We must wear the
Coat of arms and extend ourselves past our own
Worries and help rebuild this nation.
We must never forget the 144,000
Buried beneath Iwa's waters.
We must dance in the rebel
Footsteps of Petro
Place love back deep into our
People's history.
We must prove.
L'union Fait La Force
Unity makes strength
& the fragility of freedom is always
worth the fight.

for **tea**

It wld only seem fitting that the questioning of
my growing
older wld come to me at a trader joe's in the
suburbs of Michigan.

The state i was born in. 1971.
there i was. buying organic. just home
from Europe. and newly locked hair still growing under
a sideways brim. my companion gets to the free coffee
in dixie cups first.

I don't feel old. I feel clear and more confident than I
ever was in my twenty year old body.

He traveled, like us, far away from the perimeter
of Detroit to buy healthy packaged food.

He is a new vegan and is carrying a lone half gallon
of TJ soy vanilla in a mint green and white tub
dripping slightly
it melts, like skin.

It is cold like a man
who never felt love
from a woman.
I see the boy in his eyes
and search in my head wildly
for a girl to introduce him 2.

I pull a weeping willow from his eyelash
and tease my old friend about how revolutionary
his spirit was on our college campus.

Now I need a nap and I gotta go to work. He said.

We laugh.

We are surrounded by gluten free syrups
and non brand name cereals.

My family doesn't know how to bring themselves
to call this food, food. There isn't enough
blood on it.

George Zimmerman was finally arrested. Second degree
Murder. We speak as if the hippie shoppers don't exist.

We sound old, talking about how the new generation
doesn't understand the work, the organizing we did all
the way back in the day
in the nineties.

Some of us still alive.
I half laugh & try not to listen to these
nearly 40 year old men converse about the "new crop."

Tuning in costs me $35 extra in groceries i don't need.
Dark Chocolate with black sea salt bar,
brie cheese (not quite vegan)
and salt and pepper addictive chips.

My grown up junk is refined. i don't buy kid candy anymore.
The new "crop" is not the soybean. it is the 22 year old girl.

"Wait till the men stop looking your way, then you'll feel it."
He says it as a promise. A threat.

I am frozen in the non frozen section. Near the check out.
I am not ready to check out.

So many of the young one's are always
checking me out.

Give it 8 years.

He gave my vanity a death sentence.
there it was. the loneliness of sugar. the drive to find comfort
far away from home. Just a little company.
I want to hug my dear friend and tell him.

Women spend their whole lives with men watching them.
Groping, complimenting, touching, raping, sizing up.

I think the first time i caught a man's eye i was 4 or 5.
He thought my dress was pretty.
He played itsy bitsy spider up my back with his fingers.
He never hurt me but i remember never wanting to be near him
when he came back to do the lawn work. He was a long haired dirty
man I used to fantasize about
stabbing his eyes out so he couldn't look at me or none
of my pretty dresses

The objectification of my underdeveloped 11-year old body,
in junior high length shorts and baseball cleats could turn the head
of a predator. If I cld burn off the eyes of men off my body
like leaches. The white boys who sneaked to look in catholic school.
The old men, my daddy's friends, the men at the corner liquor stores.
If I cld remove the eyes of men for 50 more years maybe I cld
sleep in peace. If men suddenly turned blind when i was simply
putting gas in my car or walking with my son in the park on a sunny
day, without me feeling like i may be kidnapped or pulled into an
alley or when eyes are pulling off my clothes as i ride my bike.

Some girls realize they are beautiful at knife point.
Their beauty punched down their own throats. Ripped from inside
out.

They can no longer birth another baby girl reflection.
A wld be daughter she will pray is not
too pretty too soon
that her breasts stay pancake flat till she's 12
to avoid danger.

We with our power in pigtails.
We who send boys running in circles
and fighting for the first dance.
There is something to be said for the daughters of
Haki's yellow-black mothers.
Some of us can't wait to be ignored. to simply be left alone.
Those of us who found self love inside revolutionary text, songs
& vines of stretch marks anointing us into motherhood.

I have no interest in boys or interns.
Vegan ice cream or being 25. again.
Some of us knew we were beautiful
long before any man
ever told us.

flawless

for the man with my first son's name
Omari Hardwick

you say the fresh mint tea is
flawless. & i want to tell you
so is your smile. but everyone
tells you that. so instead i listen
to your animated stories about
life. we both southern & east coast.

we share poems. talk about love
& politics & the things we've
lost. we. comfortable as Baraka
in Newark/speaking to Sonia in her
home in Philly. poets who loved
the movement. the possibility of
words having power.

i am reminded of why i fell in love
so many times in brooklyn. with poets.
with moments. with heated debates.
with thinking people. why sometimes
i felt like that scene died & what was
born just didn't feel authentic enough
for me to still participate.

i was already famous. too soon.
never famous. enough.

i watch you demonstrate the way
a man needs to stand when he stands
next to a sista like me.

i ask you to find this man, &
bring him to me. you can't find him

in your head quickly. & i like
most women like me resign myself
to being josephine baker with many lovers
& a table full of rainbow children we love
even if we didn't birth them.

i listen to you tell me. about me.
the way i point out the surroundings.
an over-exited tour guide. so excited
to show someone me, let alone my home.

i want to tell you how much i know death.
but i can't. i can see the pain beneath those
long lashes & boyish grin.

no. i've never lost a child. but i have lost a child.
with your name. i was told to bury him & i didn't
know the process. a burial of a child that is not dead
is not possible. but it happens.

with paperwork & egos.
& no one sends you flowers or hallmark cards
when you lose this way.
cause they never respected your work
outside the womb.

i want to find a way to tell you
that i came home to bury one of the loves of my life.
in 2007.
my best friend yale miller. my teacher & brother
who protected me for years.
through prayers & the possibility that there were
still real men like him

on the planet.
i hated this city that you can love enough

while you are here briefly enough
to still see stars sparkle at the still of night.

i've watched this dark city eat my friends. like Lions.
bleed them till there wasn't nothing left but dormant
skin & bone.

my brothers. men. striped Tigers. i loved. died here.
it's the reason i'm afraid to raise my King here.
& i wonder if i'll ever find my King.
here?

i am a consummate detroit widow. refusing to wear black.
writing obituaries & poems for my 17 year old niece.
beaten to death across the street from my high school
neighborhood. just weeks ago. that dress just home
from the cleaners.

joy road. i want to drive you up this street i walked
to get to my high school.
to see how much happiness has been sucked from
her corners.
the same corner i found Ntozake Shange on.

i don't know how to truly explain
that i understand the depth
of your pain. Uncle Kenny. that i have outlived death
the same way your father did after being shot five times
that all my girls have had guns to their heads. that we have
been a city under fire long before any recession. that we have
been outliving death since birth.

i've been burying my friends since i was 16 years old.
not everyone knows what that feels like.

there are no magic words to explain why

i will forever carry the sadness
of losing my spiritual
brother Hassan/taken from us/when he was already
confined to a
wheel chair.

that he was my only friend that called daily
when i moved back to this city after 12 years
to ask about my heart.
said none of them   were jesstifyable

enough for me.

i'm ashamed of my curses to God. i want to tell you i am
a thorn. i just smile like a rose. i suppose. that i am broken.
slightly. growing. writing. still writing like that 20- year old
girl on the couch of my best friend charlotte's house.
writing a poem that wld forever change my life
when they heard it on 125th street on that stage
that looks so big on t.v./on that show that wasn't
about poetry. but it was.

this beautiful/dangerous place will make you feel an
uneasy/safeness

right before winter.

it will trick you into loving her in French.
have you buying her homes before the temperature really
drops. the sky turns silver
& everything turns cold.

the best thing that has happened to me in October
besides being introduced to the Nancy Wilson record
I've Never Been to Me

& re-finding my teenage friend who has the best
medicinal marijuana in the midwest
& watching my son write all five of his names
with kindergarten ease

has been you.

helping me find the joy   in my city again.

to lie down on the ground of my artists/friends work. on
Heidelberg & Mt. Elliot & actually see
it for the millionth first time.

to see my son nervous & excited to meet someone
when he is usually confident.

& for you not to waiver & make me feel embarrassed
when he asked

"are u gonna marry him?"

& i laugh & say "No"
but i will write him a poem King
since he wrote one for us
before he ever knew us.
& you were inside of me.
brewing.
like honey & fresh mint leaves
& afternoon tea.
life is.

flawless.

When **Poets**

When the farmer is obsolete
When the worker is no longer the core
Of this new America

I will lick the open wounds
At wound/ed knee
I will swallow freedom
Bury it deep like a depressed
Break beat waiting for
His mother to return
Home from her long ride
From Motown to the Bronx.

Jay Dee's East Side basement
Studio is a people mover/ A train
Stop. You in your tracks. Hip Hop

Didn't we?

With emancipated heat. With steel heart. With integrity.
With that gentle shit in your gut you can only
Get from the beautiful gutter.

I will find the trail of tears
Along my tired spine
And drink the chocolate blood
Of this land.
So sweet and bitter on my tongue.
This bastard language.   Of my home.

My enemy happens to be the
love   of my life.

I will trace my DNA to the Moors of Spain
Who conquered my European Ancestors

Me trying to kill me.

Still left breathing
Inside
I will bake in the sky that lies to clouds

I will worship cows and eat purple flowers.
I will eat music rising. Write poems with
Pale snow in the middle of June.

When all the poets have died
Or become actors.
When the poets laugh on cue.

When words turn obsolete
When love is an idea not an action
When romance is reduced to scheduled
Weekends.
When men don't want to kiss
Beautiful women
In the bright of the sun.

When I am uninspired to write
Poems about being un/inspired to write.
When my artist heart stops seeing the
Beauty and stories in strangers.

When they silence all the revolutionaries
When innocent men are murdered
On a world stage.

When dream cries.

When the rich actually believe they
Are the chosen people.
When the Motor City runs out of cars and
People who love winter.

The oppressed do not need to be saved
By the philanthropist/the national organizer

We are our own best kept secret.
We are the rescued.
We are the well endowed.
We are the miracle of what was
Taken. The map Harriet left behind.

We are yellow Michigan leaves falling
humbly/ holding onto October.
Blowing a breath of soul out of our
Horned mouths.

The inevitable cold.
Always coming.

We our own Jesus people.
We are the Midwest city Allah's children
Call home outside the East.
We are the spirit of the forsaken.
We are the graves they will love to
Walk over.

When the poets dress the part.
When the poets forget to drop
Bombs not metaphors.

I will lie down my pen.
I will lie with this pen.
I am writing this on a MAC.

This is not writing.

Maybe this is the end of literature
When you can only find poems on/line
When ink has turned to water.

When the poets.
When the poets.

When the poet is obsolete.
One day the young ones will become the pioneer.
The elders become the ancestor.

We live for this day.
We die a little on this day.

When the poets forget.
When the poets put down their weapons.
When the poets forget to love.

When the poets are in fashion.
Drink in French and write
With fear.

What will I wear
What will I wear

Becomes more important

Than what will I say.
What will I write.
How will I make these words

Food.
Shelter.
Truth.

How will I tell my son
Mommy was a poet.
And let that mean
Any damn thing. At all.

When the poets.
When the poets.

When artists.
When mothers.
When lovers
When liars
When movements
When people
When history
When poets.

When

?

a poem saved my life

Homage to Detroit
for Antonio Agee aka Shades (thank you for allowing me to tell your
story & painting ours live)

They named me something French.
But I preferred Cadillac.
They didn't invite me to the naming ceremony
But they must have felt my steel body
longing for rubber against the ground.

I was re-born
The Motor City.
A beautiful city across the street from another country.
Inside a thumb surrounded by
Great Lakes.

I was music made from engines. Loud, tough.
Sometimes just a hum and hand clap sound.
When I grew up they called me

Motown.

He

is smoking a Kool Mild.
That was his way of slowing down
his 30 year old nicotine habit. For me. His second to
youngest daughter who thought he was God
and fought for position to ride in the front seat
of his white/ green
or gold Cadillacs.
Detroit daddy cool. Outside on any summer
night on the Westside with the radio loud
Enough for the entire block to listen.

And they did.
Mr. Copeland carried his front porch
chair to our driveway and they
listened to Tigers baseball on the radio.
That sound/a whisper
surrounded by a fence and a prayer.

More than fathers worshipped
by their daughters.

Men who came home to families at night
after working 12 hour days.
Blue collar Michigan men with jazz in their
feet and Motown 8 tracks in their rides.

Men who smelled like men and understood that
Women were delicate and brilliant.

Who is missing more for me than my daddy Tom Moore?
Revolutionary men who surrounded themselves
With artists and thinking people. Protesting was cool.

Plum St.
Business men. George Agee. Ran the Mystique Room
and would birth an artist who would paint the city
the bright way he saw it.
John Sinclair who incited riots and moved.
People with poems and personal transformation.
Sometimes without a flash.
Leni. Armed. Documented the action/movement. Raw.
MC 5. Rolling Stones. Pappa was.

Men.

Who made smoking. Cool. Before there was ever

A commercial campaign. Or cancer. Or non-smoking bars.
1968 Men. Hollowing out their hearts to hide their
future children from Reagan 80's invasion. Men who knew
music was power and dancing slow was an act of love.

Men on the line of assembly. Coleman A. Young men.
Fighting to desegregate fire and police departments.
Curses were like poetry when they decided to fire
back. Politics were the people's conscious and Marvin
Gaye was our battle crier.

We know work. It is our witchcraft/our bloodline gift.
Our deep south anxiety attack. Our dreams of something
greater for the ones that come later.

The men who look like daddies even when they weren't .
Dobb Hats gangstas against a snake-skin shoe.
Sunday Best men.
Saturday all night. Men.
Straight back men with pride. Organizing frontline

Union workers. Men.
Making women touch their hats and
adjust their slips
as they passed.
Construction worker with steel toed boots
and a brown bag lunch. Men.

We miss

the corner we used to safely stand on. To hear
The good gossip. The heavy fisted hand. The blue black
Detroit river of palms that carried fish to the car then to the
Crib. That's what we call it still.

missing…

The Cass Corridor Pat Halley wrote about.
Spirits of broken brick still breathing beneath the
pavement that made this city great.

He
paints in the center of this universe.
Head leaning to the right. Shades off.
Working against the same sun.
This is what sons do. Standing literally in his father's shoes.
There are no such thing as accidents.

In Islam they say the poets have angels.
Waiting at the street light. Determining the traffic.
This is how we find a way to eat. To smile.
Brush cutting through indifference. Spraying pink lips
with blue-collar edge.
Running with reckless abandon we are.
Hiding inside the intangible beauty
of rubble and rebellion.
of potholes and 24 hour Coneys.
We underground railroad survivors.
with no Union Station Downtown.

What do these artists say in a time of war?
Nobody heard a bomb drop in Detroit?
Who's pushing the buttons and spiking the tea?
We need more Word Play and cane sugar
Spray paint and pulled canvas to make the
Skyline grow.

What do we have left if not poems?
How many times would I have died
if I couldn't articulate my own existence.
What else better to feed our babies then paint?
Coughing out the muffler smoke and

running for safety from the aged meat in
what's left of the city grocery store.
We have a man made farm all over this city.
No, this is not Charles Dickens. This is
Octavia Butler and we are the chosen.
Eastern Market shoppers and young
urban gardeners. For Hire.

The art is never in the artist. It is in the
people that inspire the artists work.
So don't write Eulogies for Detroit.

No uninspired folk song of gloom.
Some of us are coming home.
To show the world
how we make
the planet move.

note: excerpted from the Detroit techno solo theater show,
The Missing Project: Pieces of the D

i **needed** to write a **love poem**

you're not my lover.
but i needed to write a love poem
so i wrote this for you.

and i know you can't be the beauty
of my mornings. know you can't
hold my body in your strumming fingers
but i needed to write a love poem
so i wrote this for you

i needed to feel that sinking
i needed the sunlight in my face
when u looked my way
needed dramatic goodbyes
& rain traveling down backs
mouths on the edge of skin
romance in hot hands in cold nights

i needed clocks stopped
& train rides through toulouse

maybe i needed   you.

i needed to pull a love poem
outta my body. put my soft heart
in a vulnerable place.

i need to hear music. be inspired by
conversation. needed your scratchy
voice in a place it doesn't belong.
in a time that doesn't exist.

i needed to be inspired by moonlight
and long walks and possibility

i needed to write a love poem.

needed to laugh in places i could never reach
needed to dance & talk & debate and paint
and write and dream

I needed desperately
to simply write a love poem

so i wrote this poem
for you.

jessica Care moore is the CEO of Moore Black Press, Executive Producer of *Black WOMEN Rock!*, and founder of the literacy-driven, Jess Care Moore Foundation. An internationally renowned poet, playwright, performance artist and producer, she is the 2013 Alain Locke Award Recipient from the Detroit Institute of Arts. moore is the author of *The Words Don't Fit in My Mouth*, *The Alphabet Verses The Ghetto*, *God is Not an American*, and *Sunlight Through Bullet Holes*. She is editing her first anthology, *Call Our Names* and writing her memoir, *Love is Not The Enemy*. She has performed her poems and solo theater shows all over the United States, in South Africa, and across Europe.

From her Broadway performances at Carnegie Hall, or Harlem's Apollo Theater, London's Institute of Contemporary Arts, to New York's Jazz at Lincoln Center, moore believes poems belong everywhere and to everyone.

She is well known for her history making, record breaking appearances on "It's Showtime at the Apollo," and is the youngest living Apollo Legend. moore's music project, *Black Tea: The Legend of Jessi James*, features Blue Note Recording artist, José James, the legendary Roy Ayers and the talented young Detroit based pianist and producer, Jon Dixon. JCM's new label, Words on Wax is partnering with legendary Submerge Records in Detroit (famous across the world for techno) to put her poetry on vinyl.

She is very proud to be Omari's earth mom and King's birth mom. Her step children were born in her heart, Kelsey, Jaden and Israel. You are all a light.

Moore Black Press Books & Authors

jessica Care moore
The Words Don't Fit in My Mouth
The Alphabet Verses The Ghetto
God is Not an American
Sunlight Through Bullet Holes

Saul Williams
The Seventh Octave

Sharrif Simmons
Fast Cities and Objects That Burn

Etan Thomas
More Than an Athlete

Ras Baraka
Black Girls Learn Love Hard

asha bandele
The Subtle Art of Breathing

Danny Simmons
I Dreamed My People Were Calling But I Couldn't Find My Way Home

Forthcoming:
Bloodlines by **Jasmine Bailey**
Call our Names - Anthology - Editor: **jessica Care moore**

www.mooreblackpress.com